NEVER FAR

from

HOME

Images from Austin

BY NICK STOCKLAND

A special thanks to Marcy McGuire for providing valuable artistic direction in the formatting of this book. This is my sixth opportunity to work with Marcy, on both children's books and photography books – two very different styles indeed. Once again her contribution is essential, and excellent.

Also a special thanks to Dionisio Manalo Jr. for an exceptional design on the book cover. This is my first opportunity to work with Dionisio, and I sincerely appreciate his contribution and artistic vision.

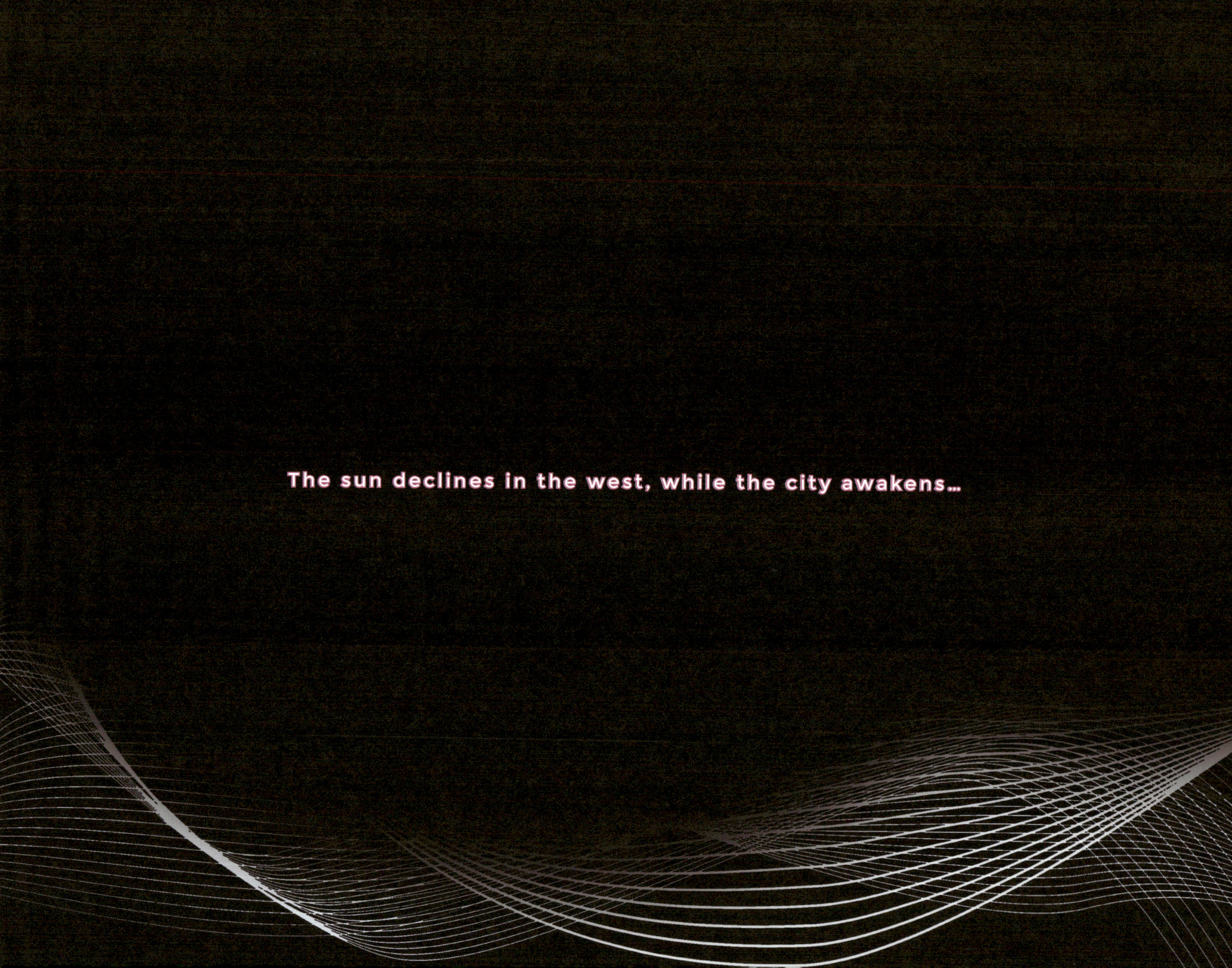

The sun declines in the west, while the city awakens…

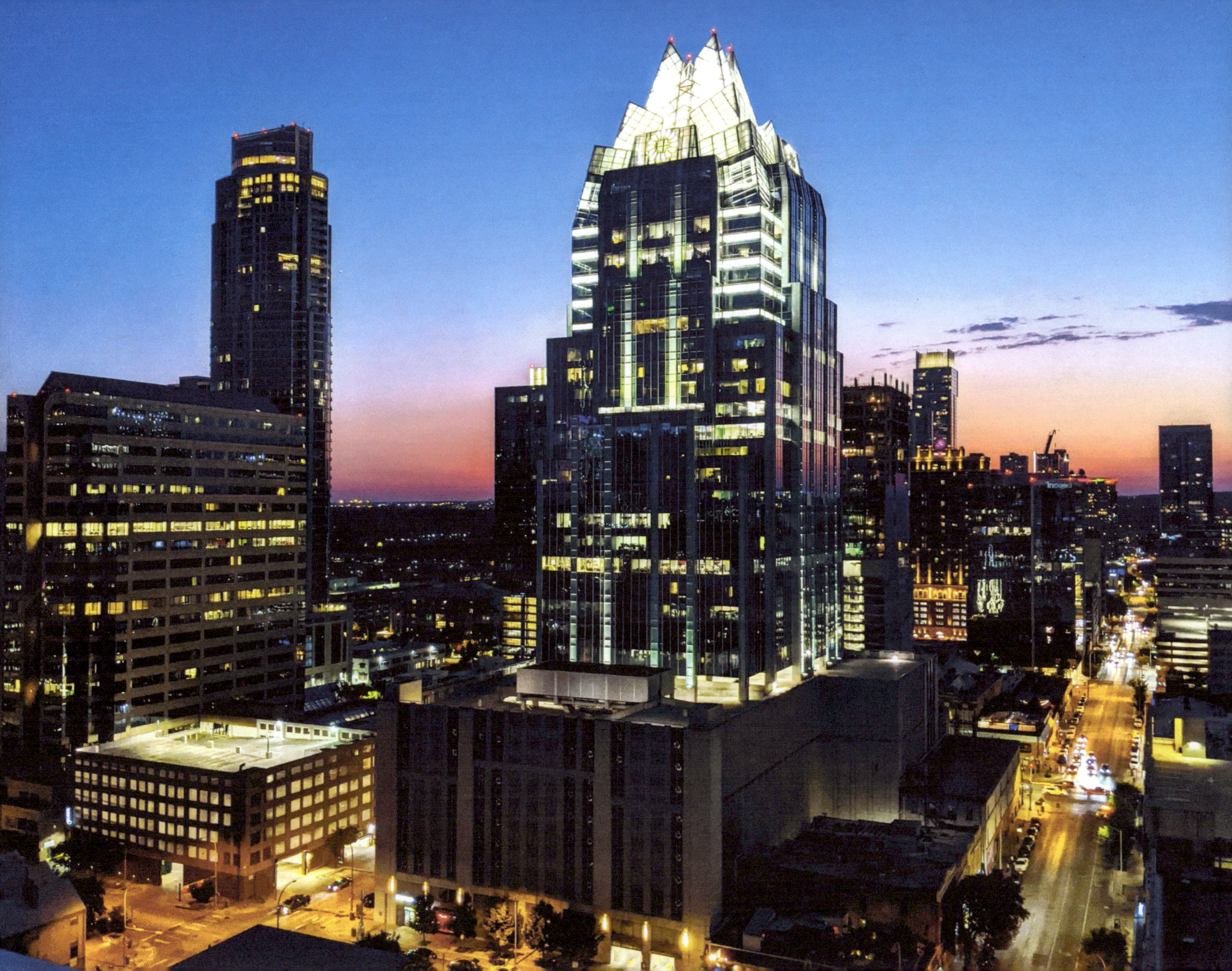

Nature has its peace, while the city has temptations…

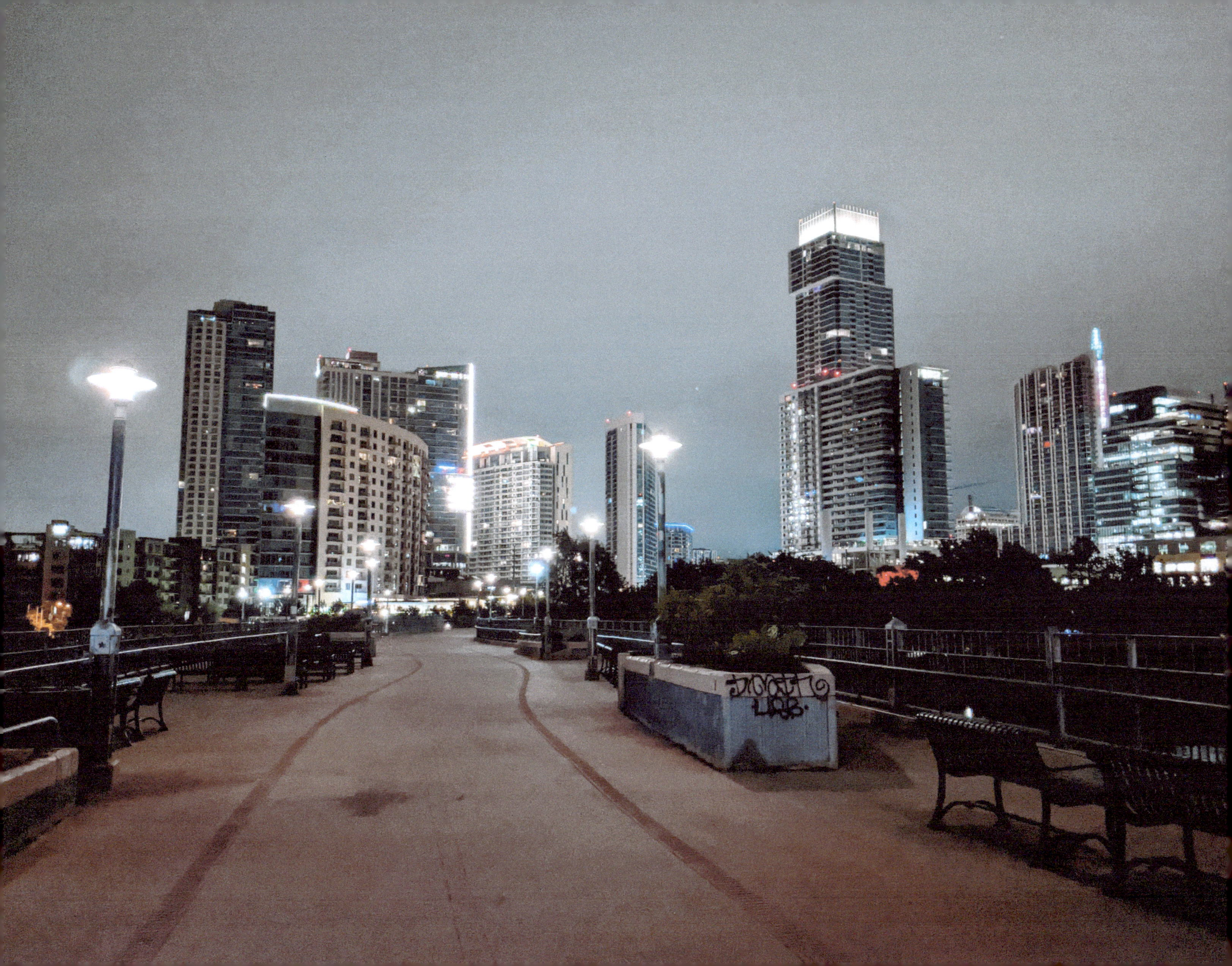

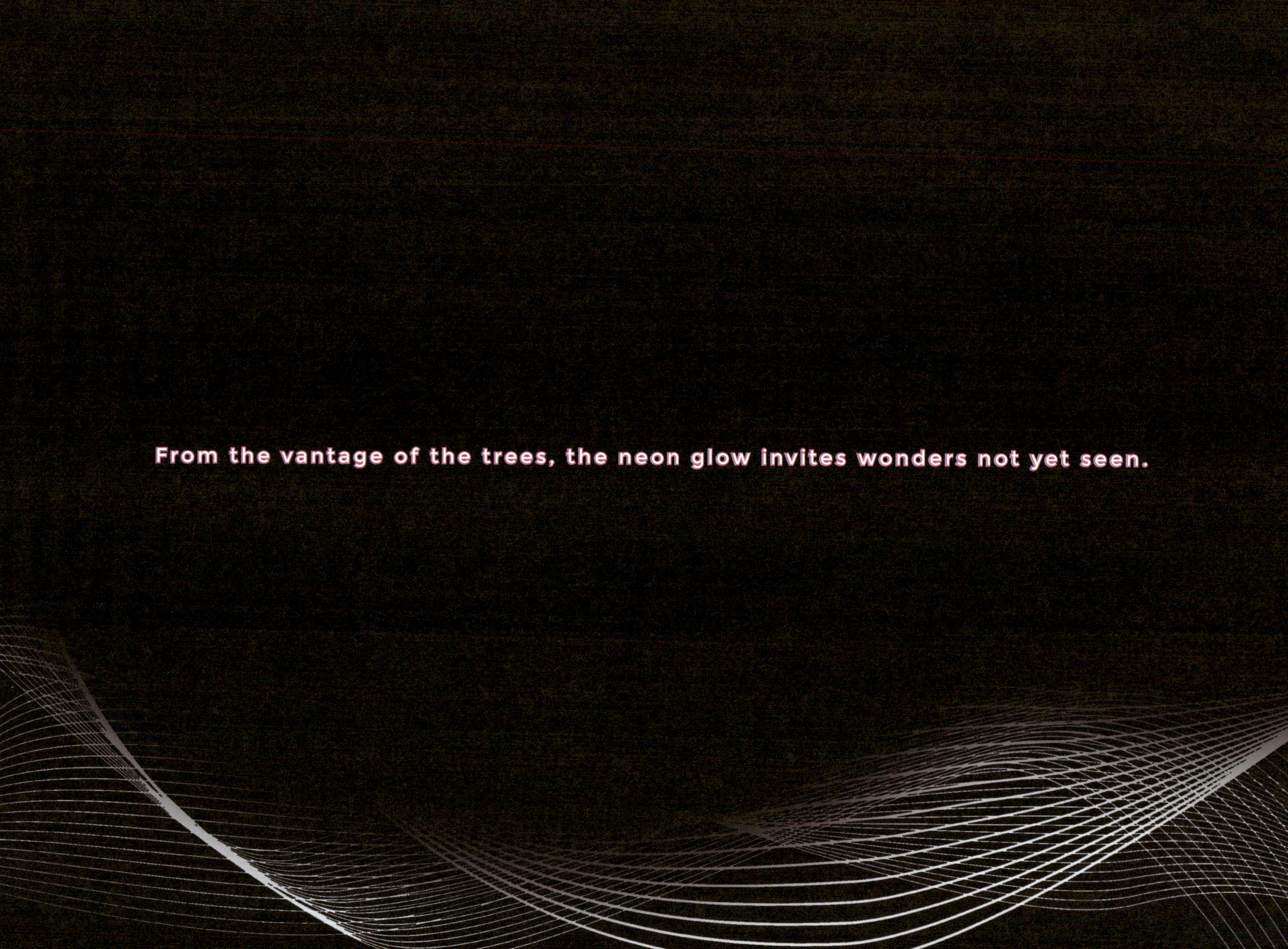
From the vantage of the trees, the neon glow invites wonders not yet seen.

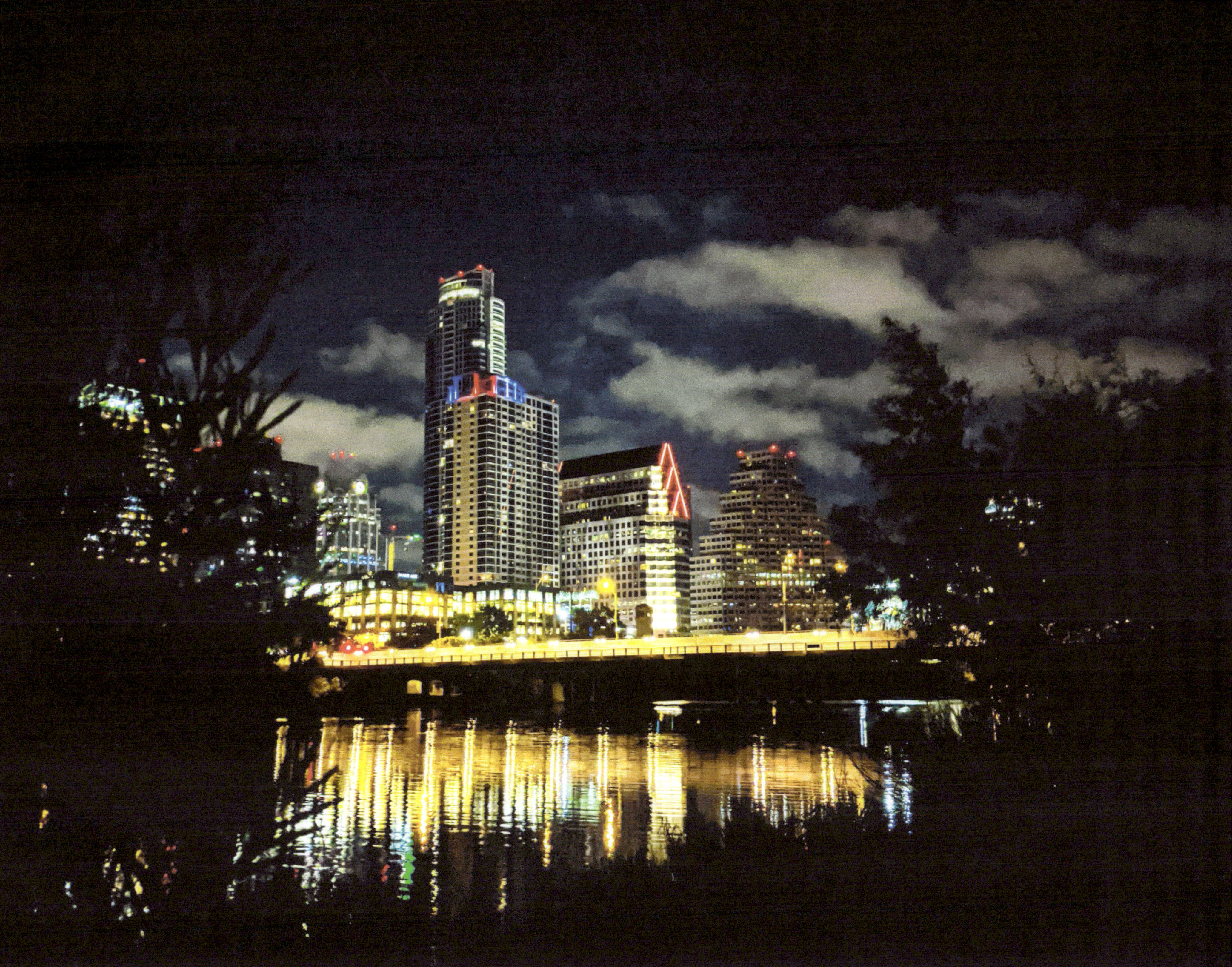

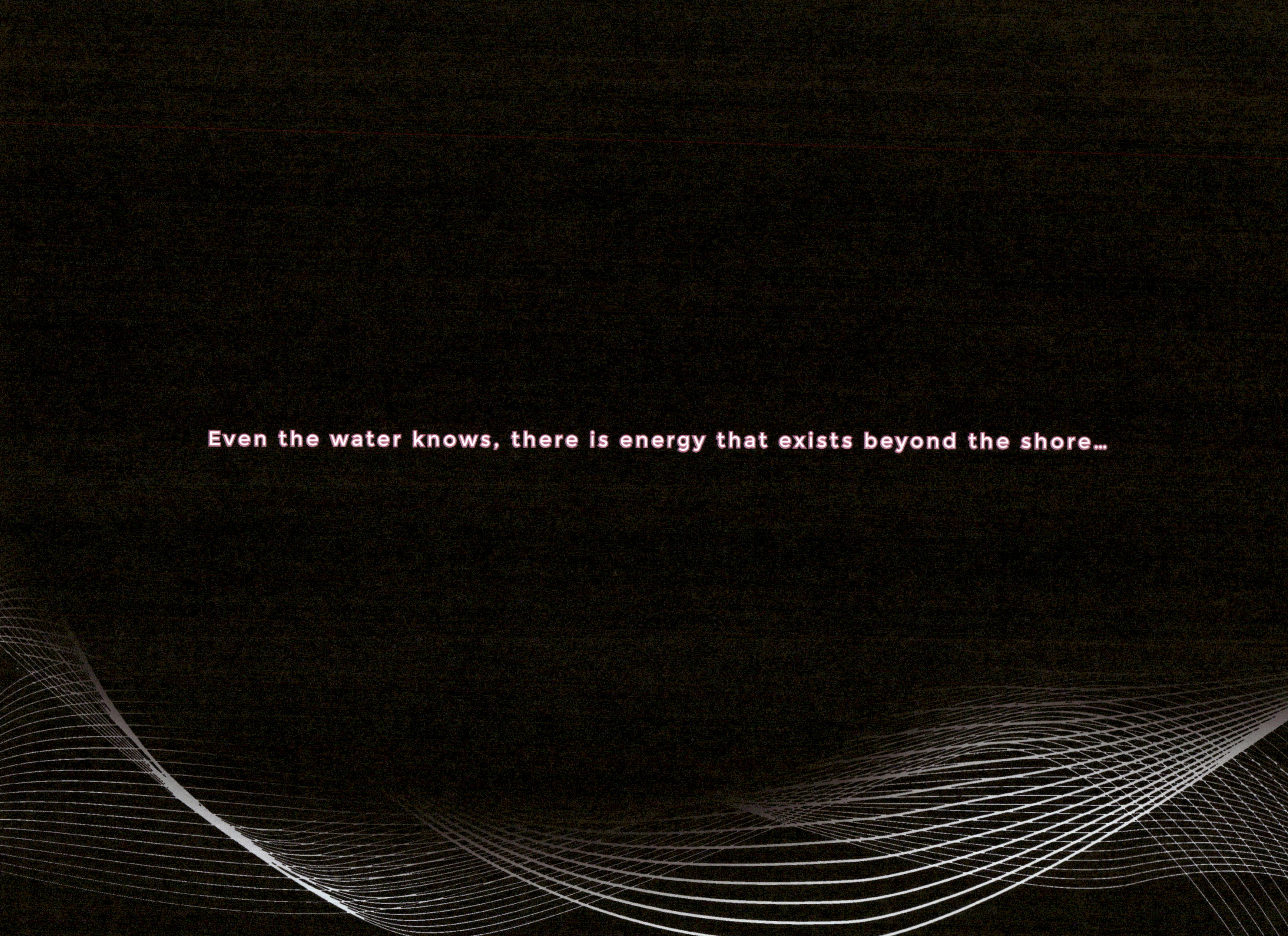

Even the water knows, there is energy that exists beyond the shore…

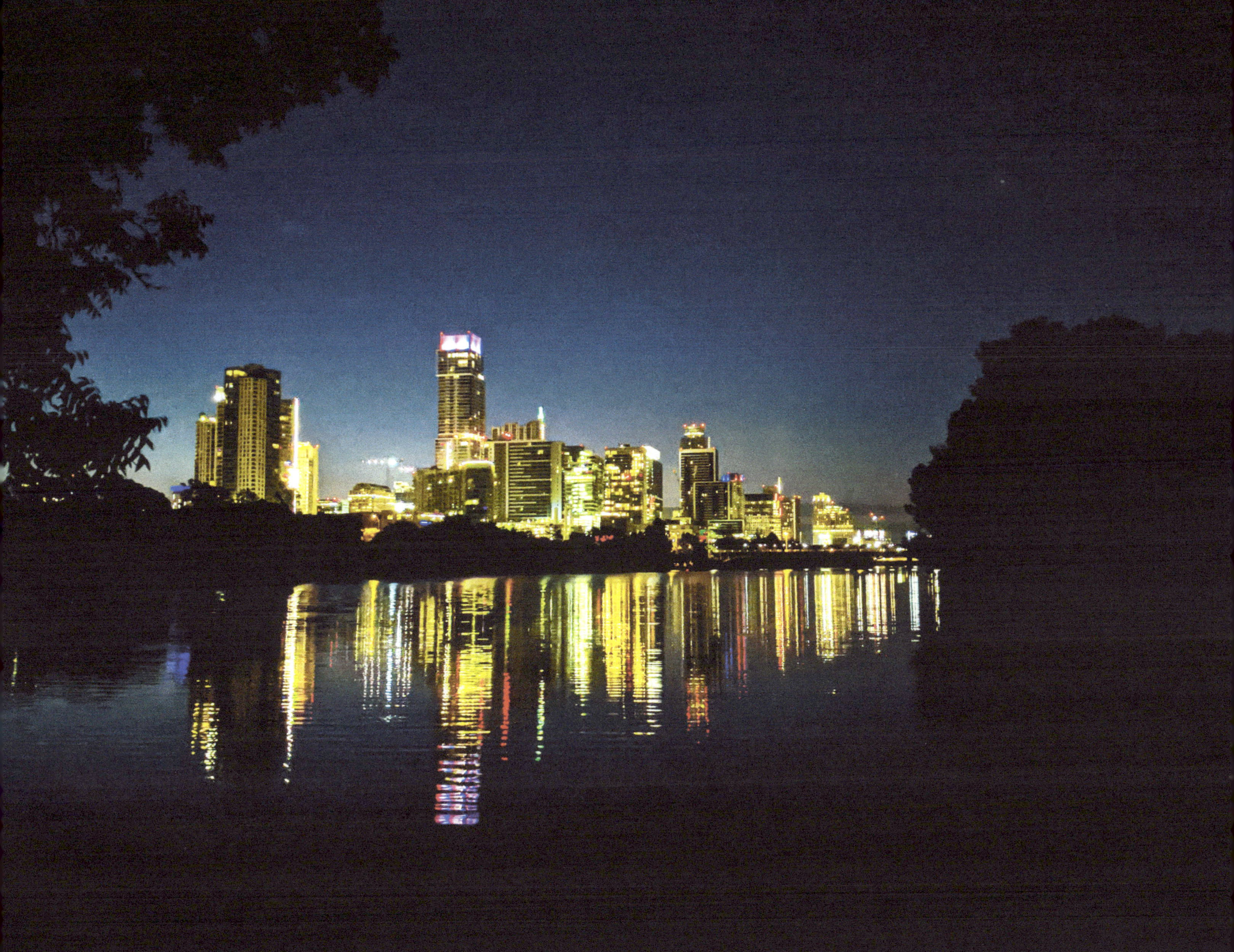

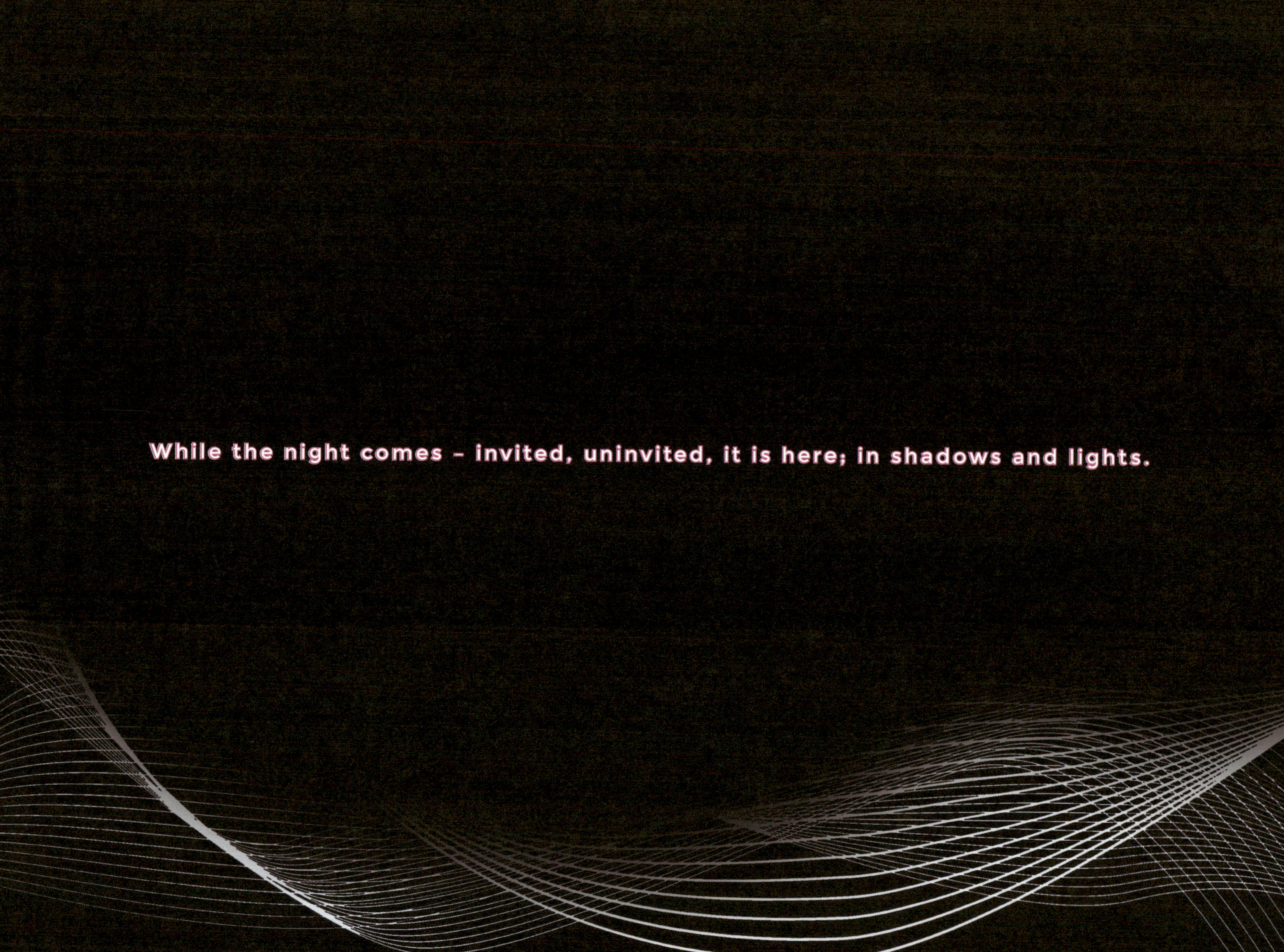
While the night comes – invited, uninvited, it is here; in shadows and lights.

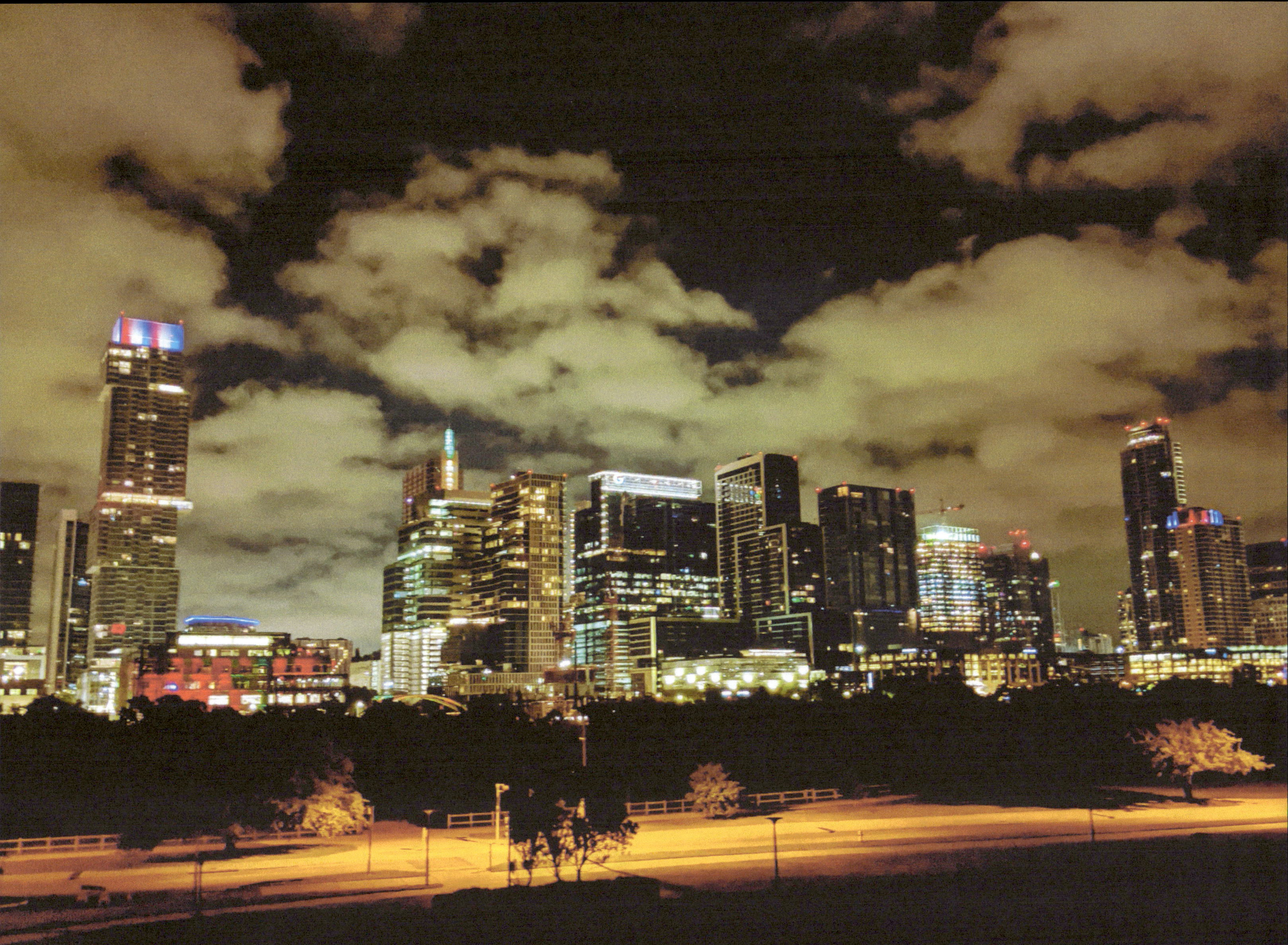

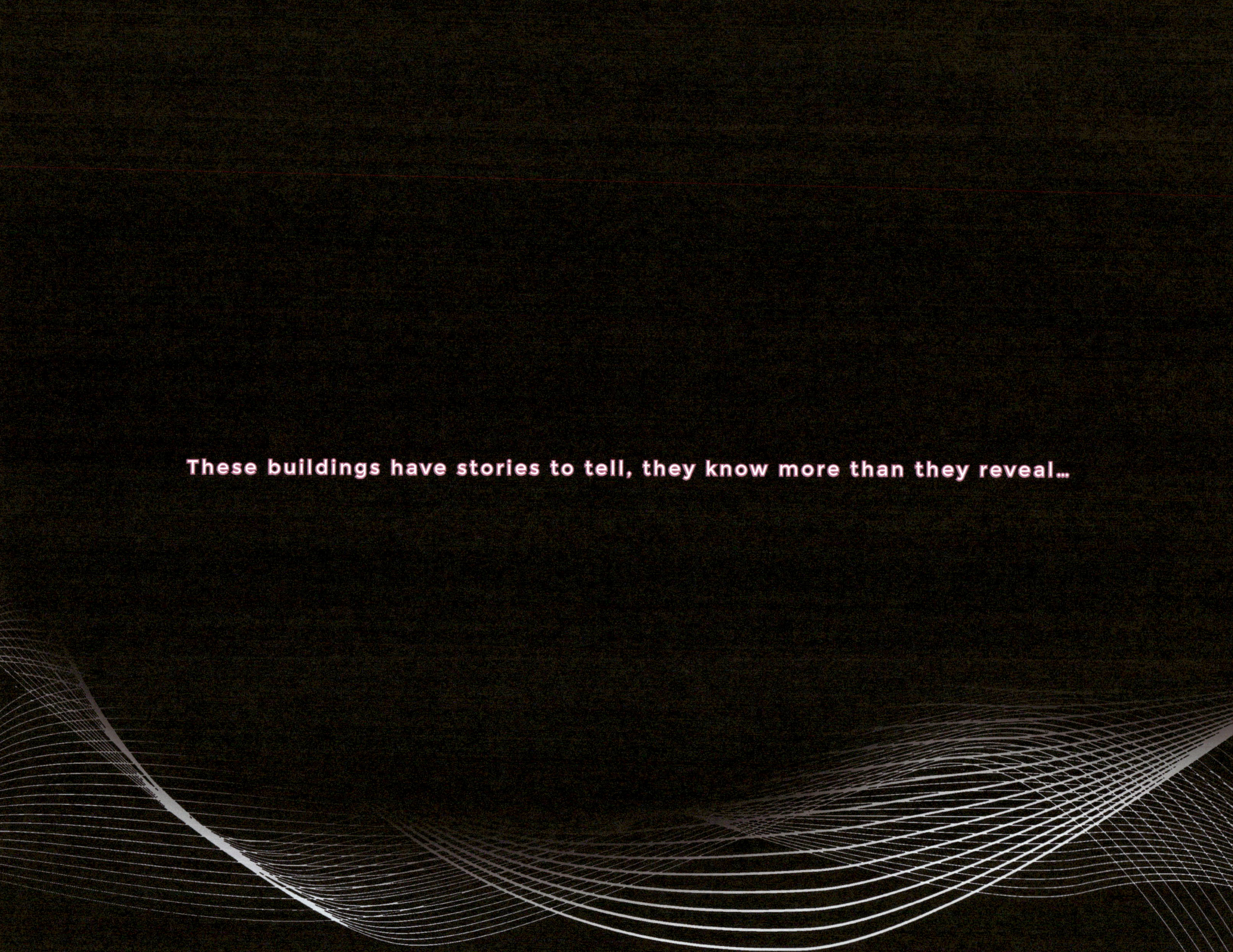
These buildings have stories to tell, they know more than they reveal…

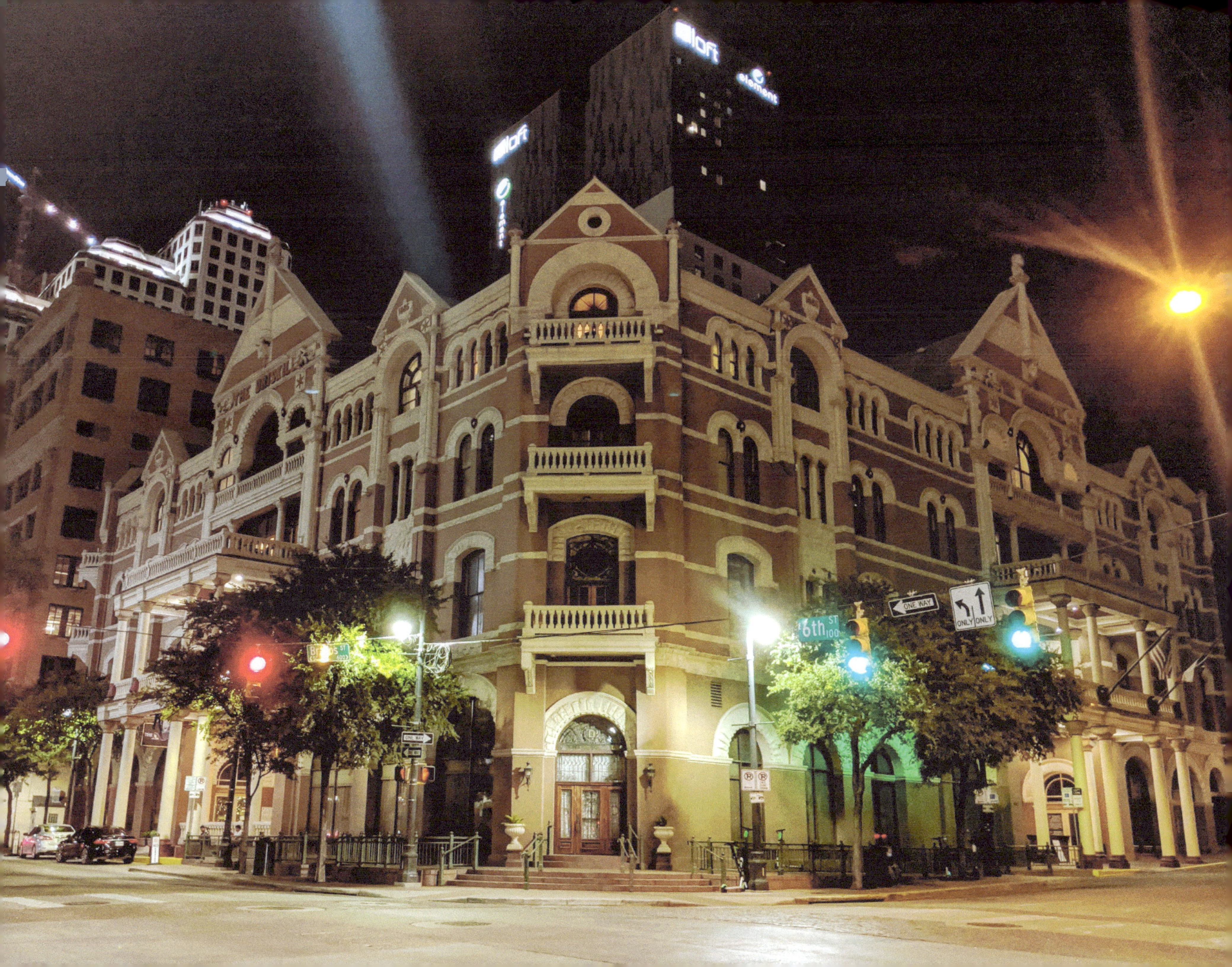

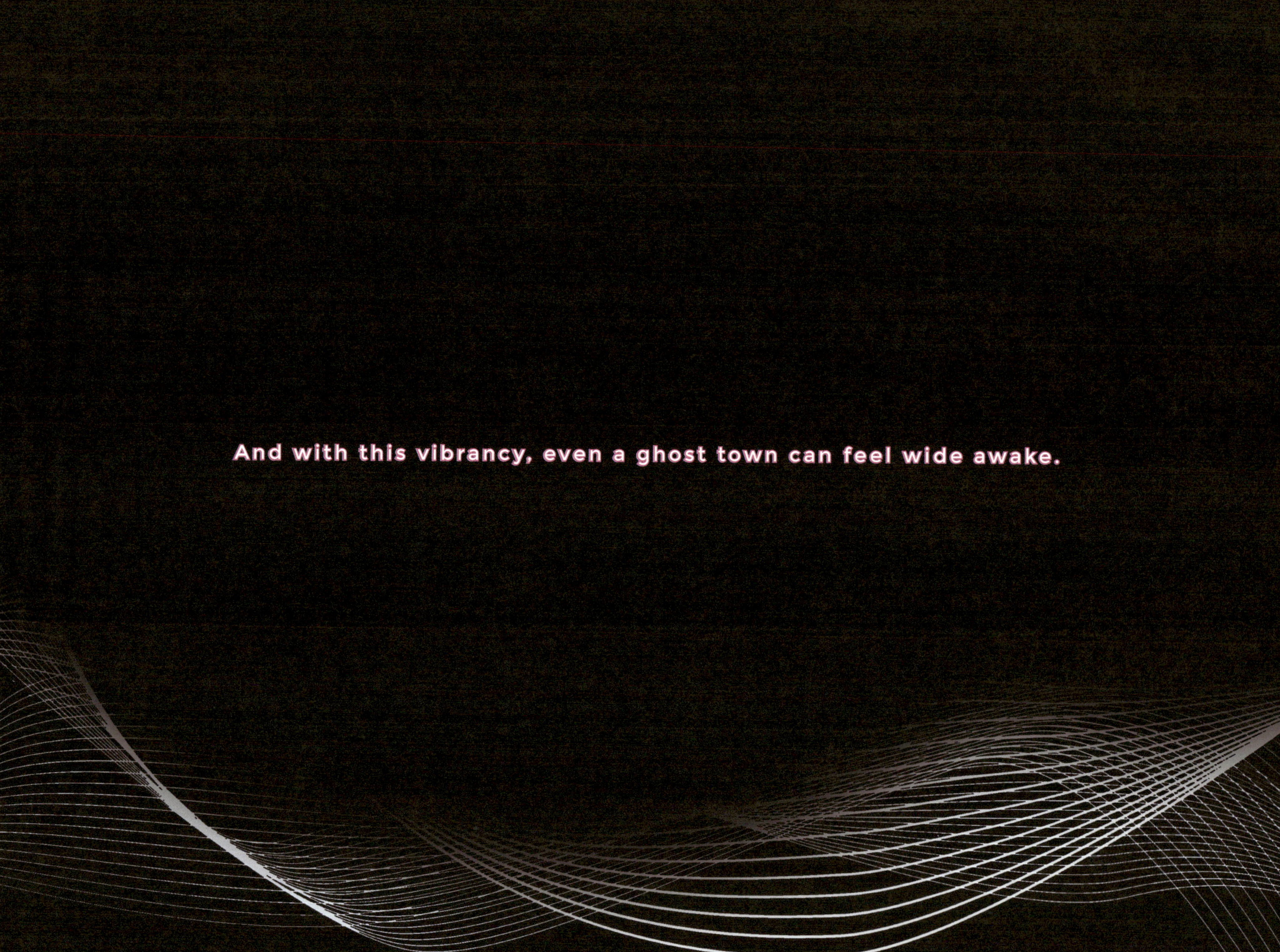

And with this vibrancy, even a ghost town can feel wide awake.

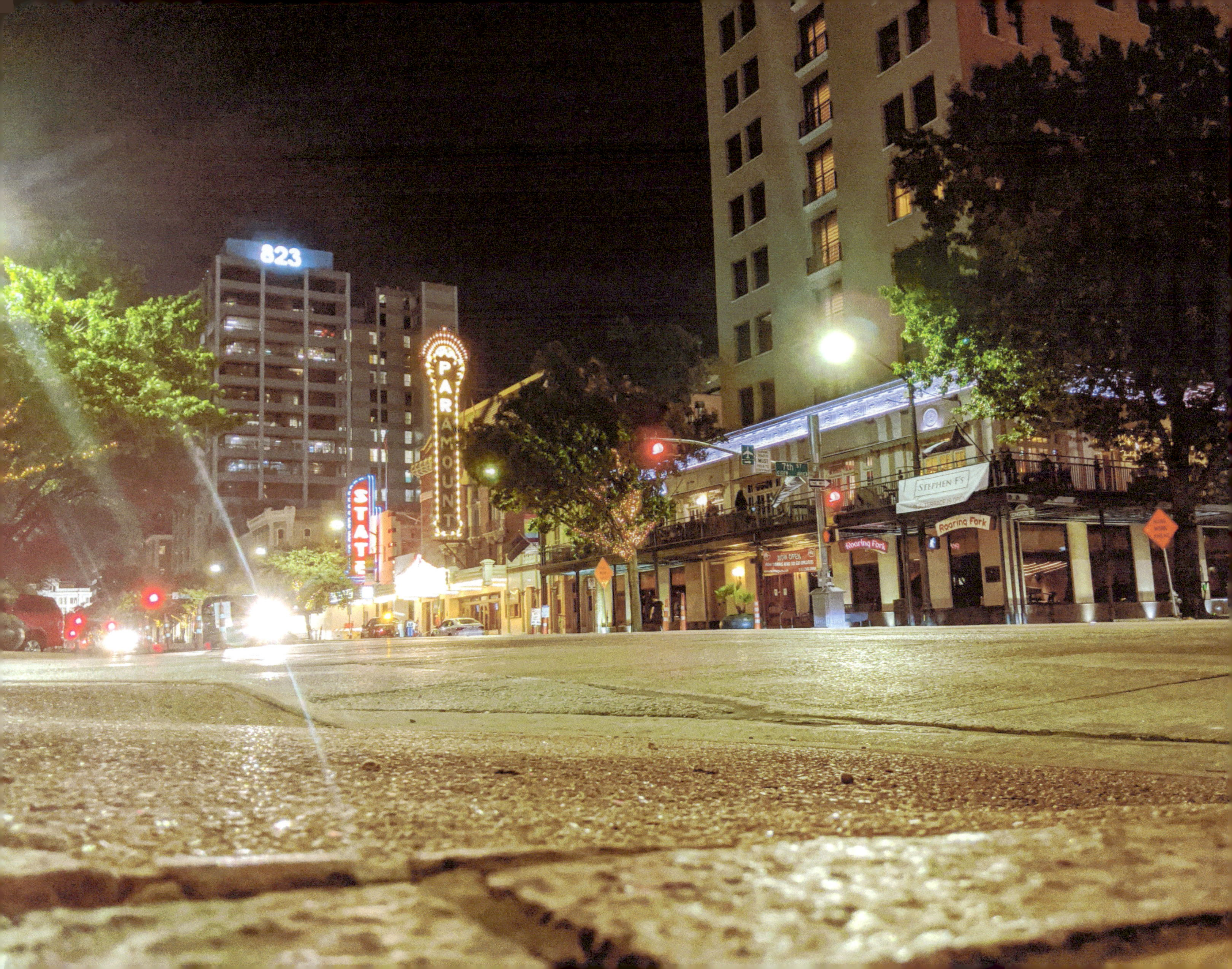
823
PARAMOUNT
STATE
STEPHEN F's
Roaring Fork
Roaring Fork
7th
NOW OPEN

These streets, where do they begin? Where do they end?

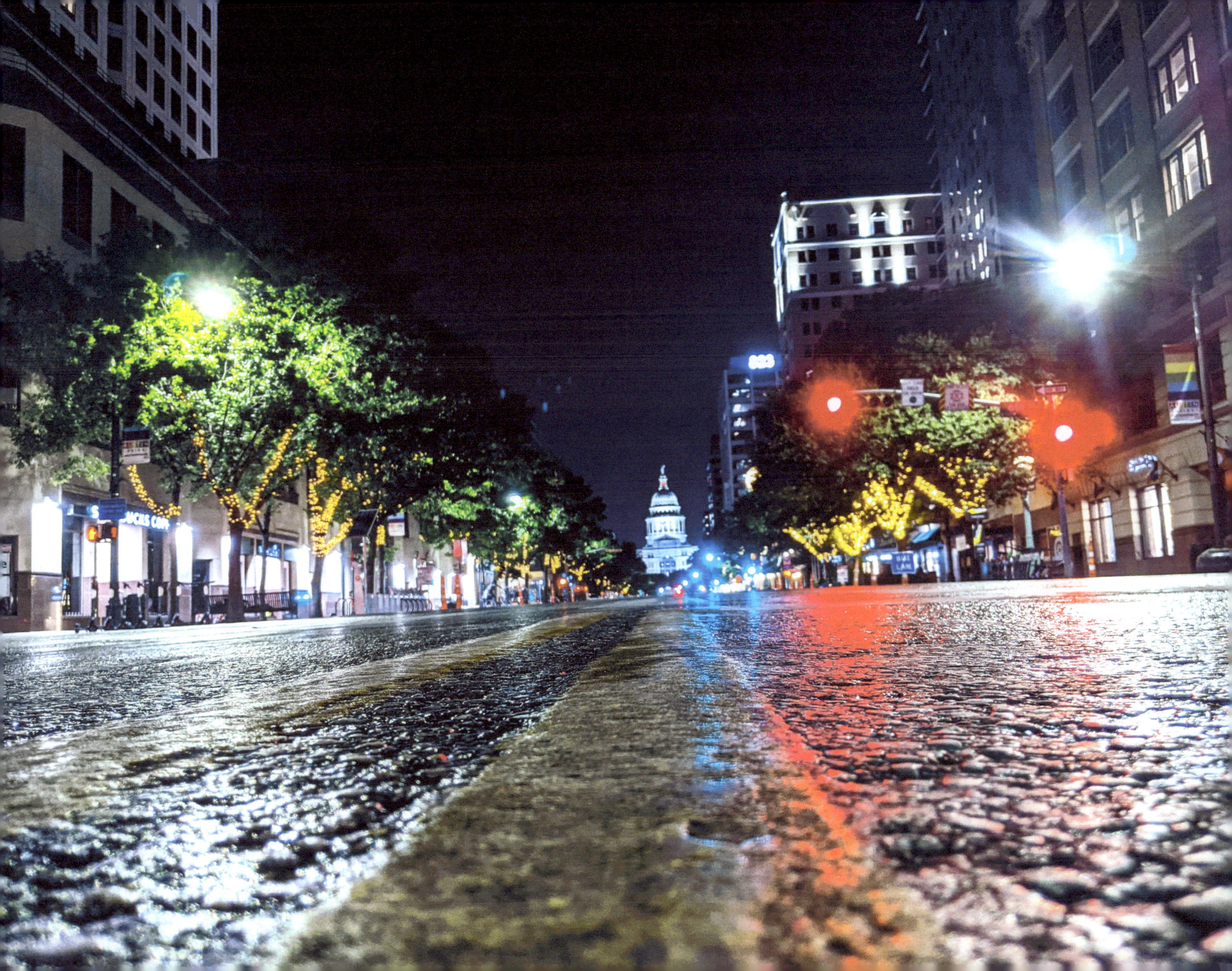

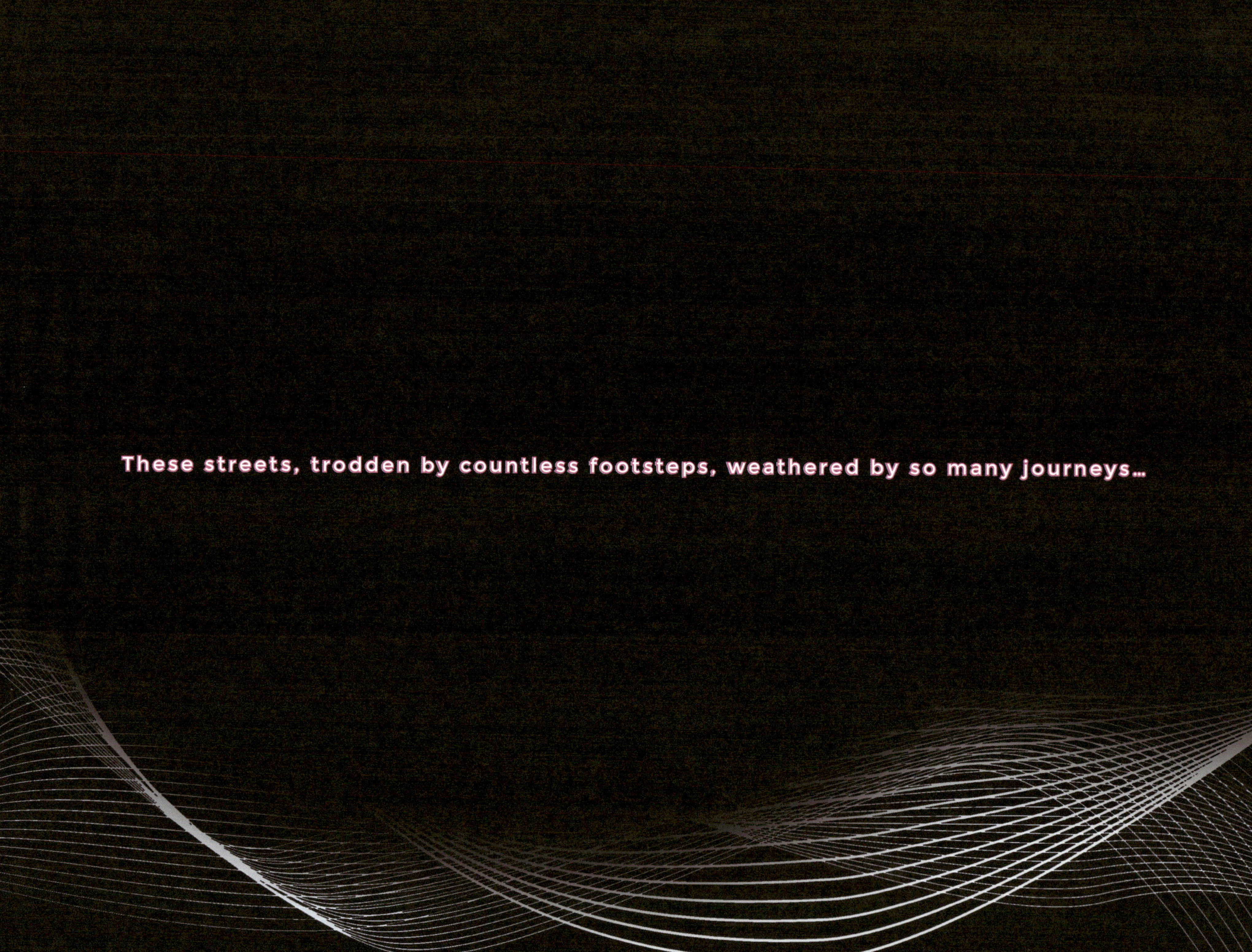
These streets, trodden by countless footsteps, weathered by so many journeys…

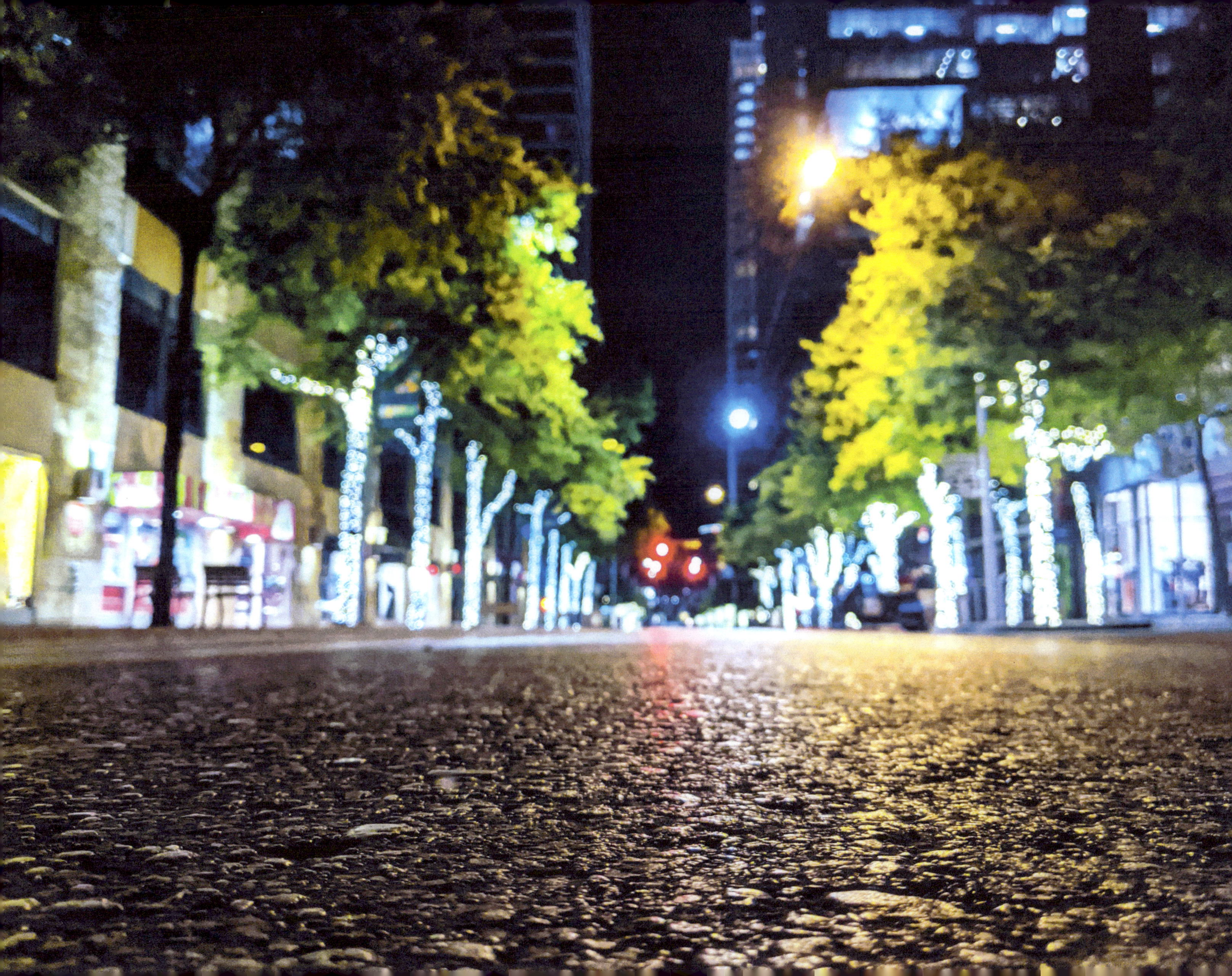

Some coming, some going, some visiting, some to never leave.

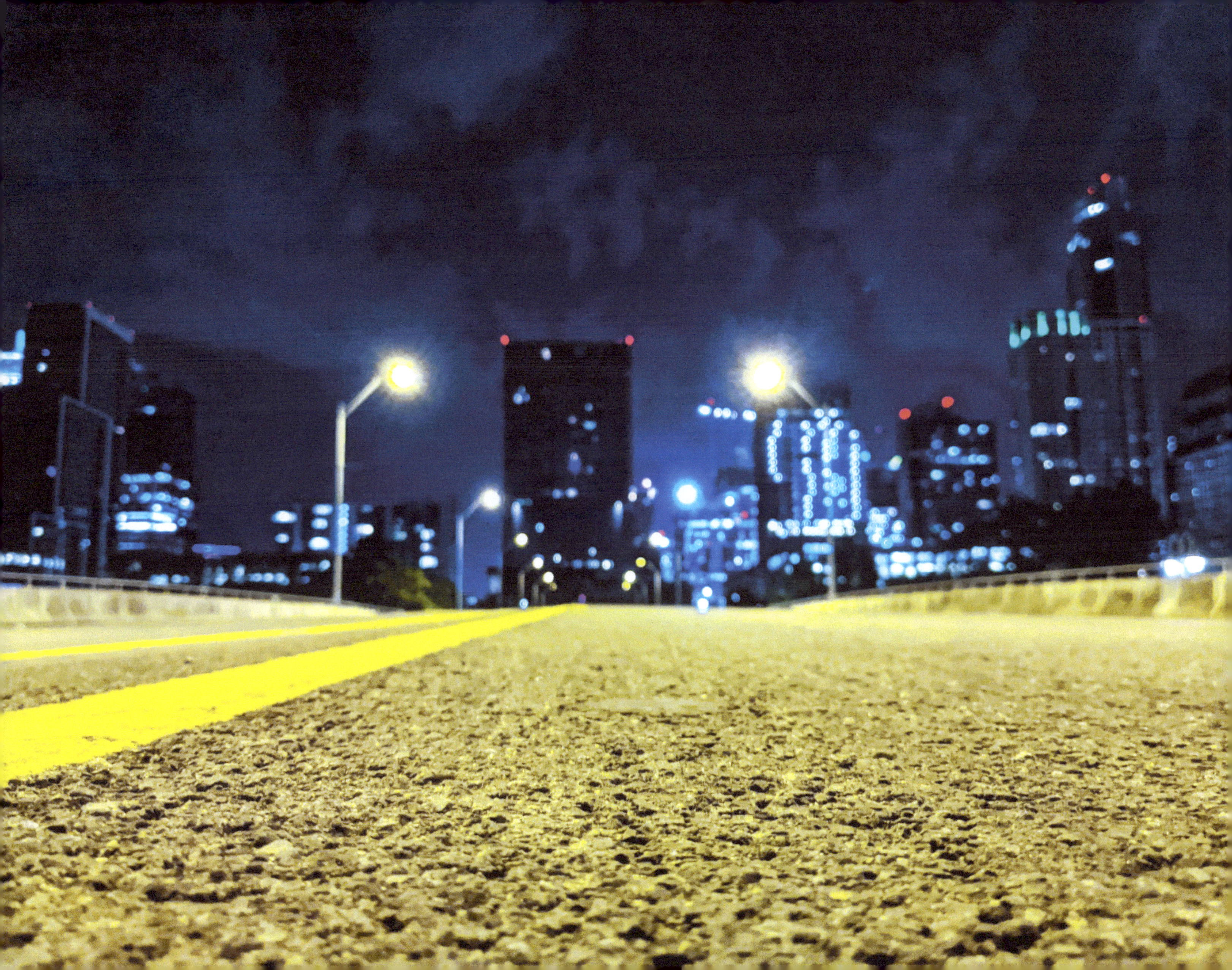

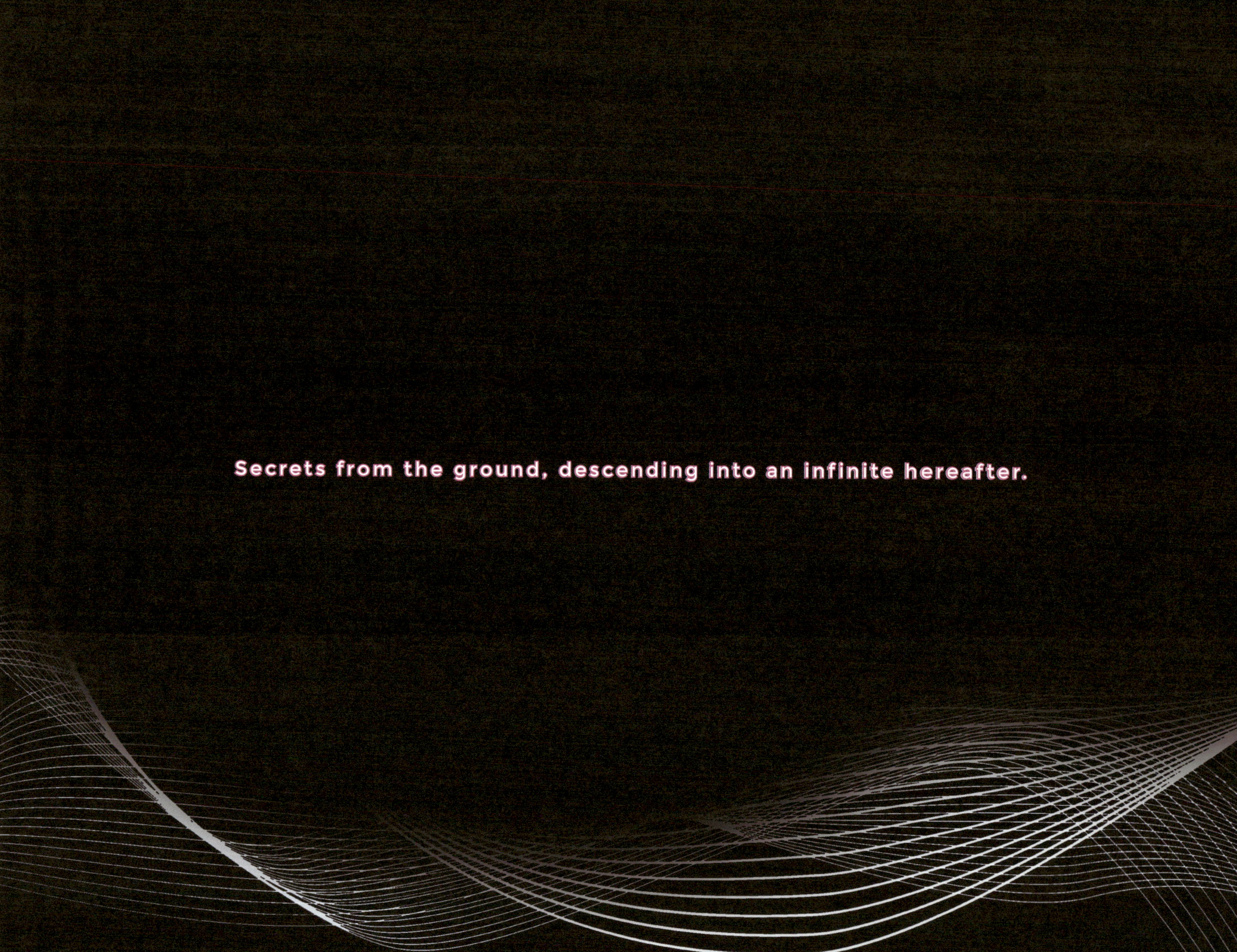

Secrets from the ground, descending into an infinite hereafter.

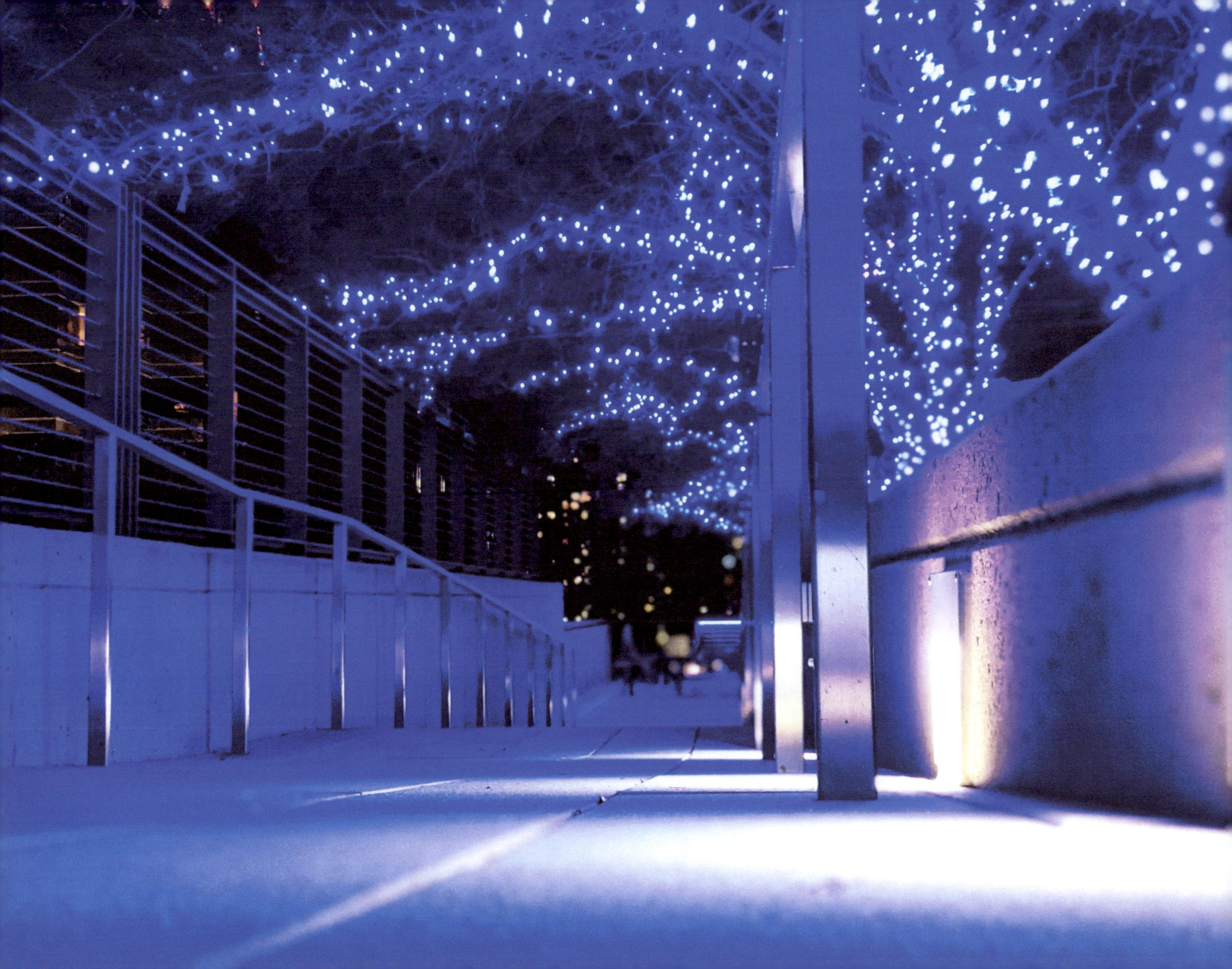

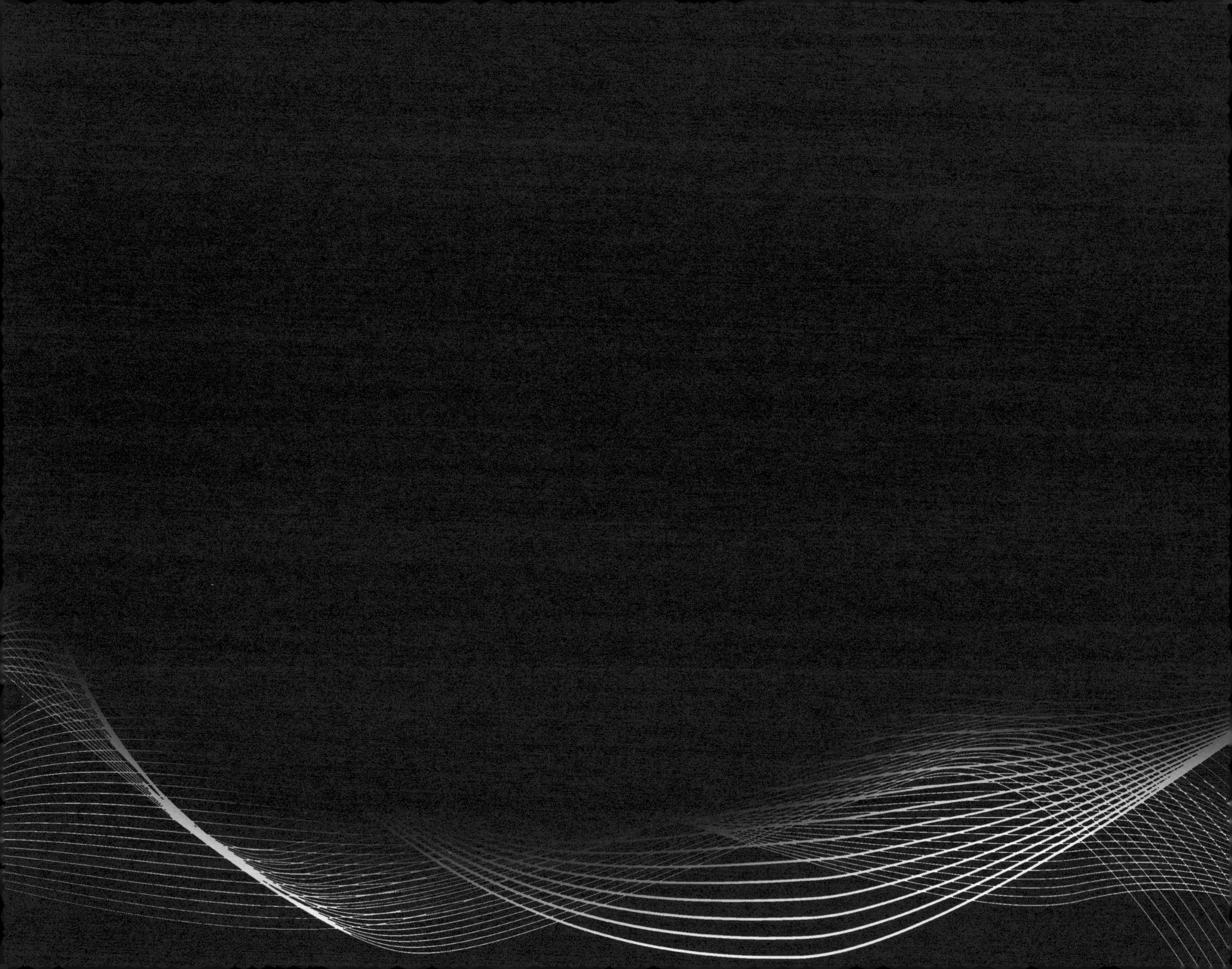

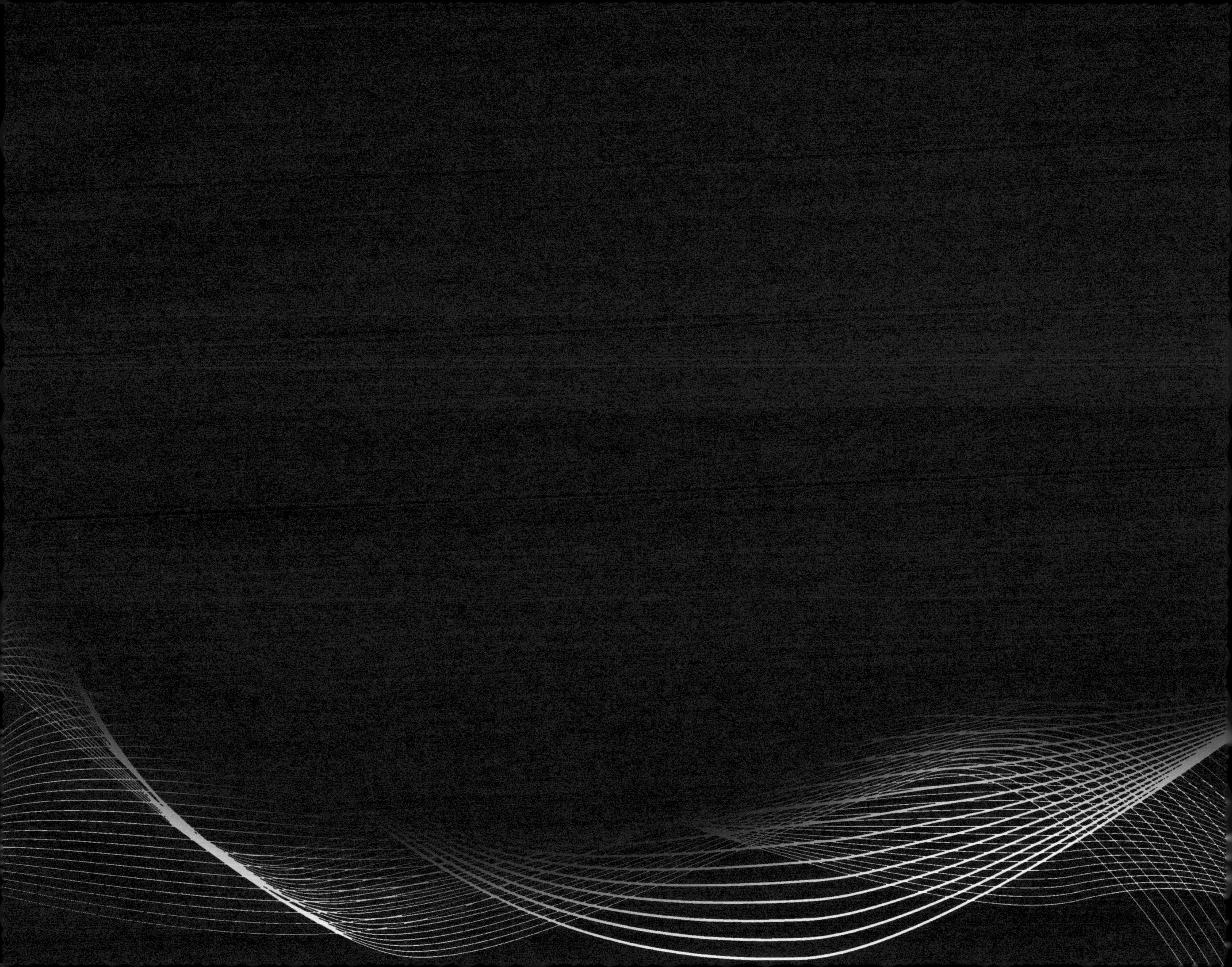

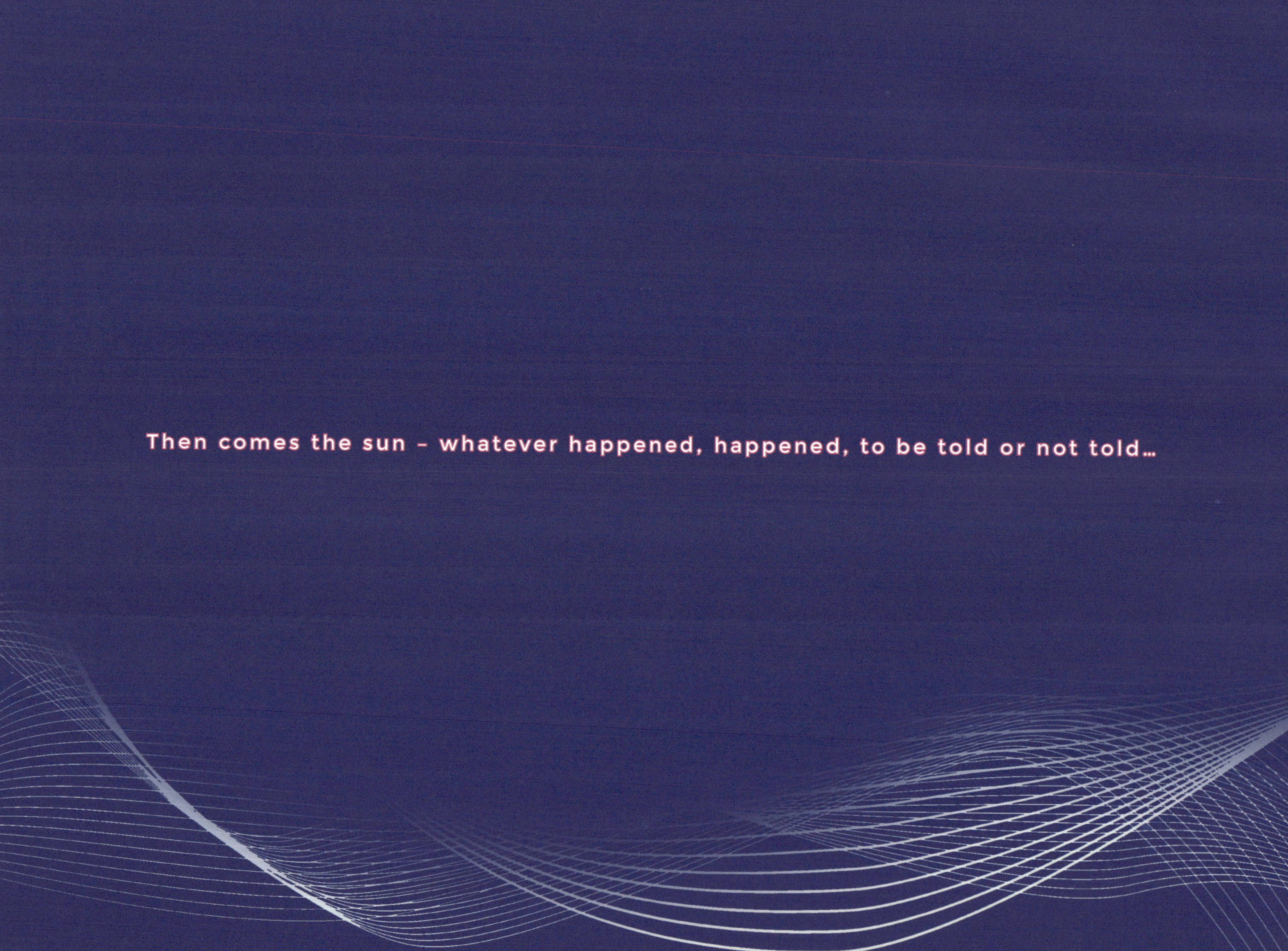

Then comes the sun – whatever happened, happened, to be told or not told…

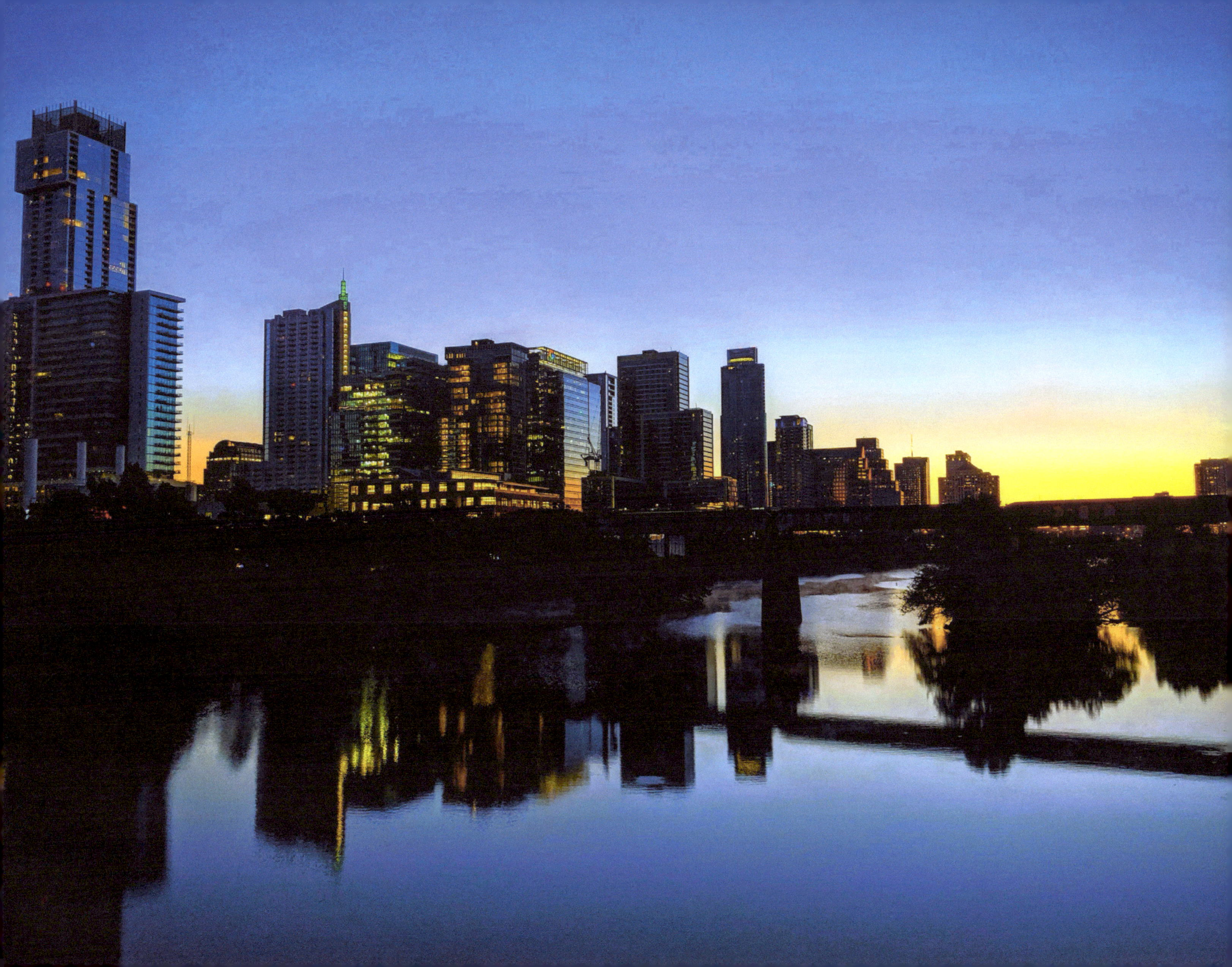

The shadows rescind, while the glow lingers for a time…

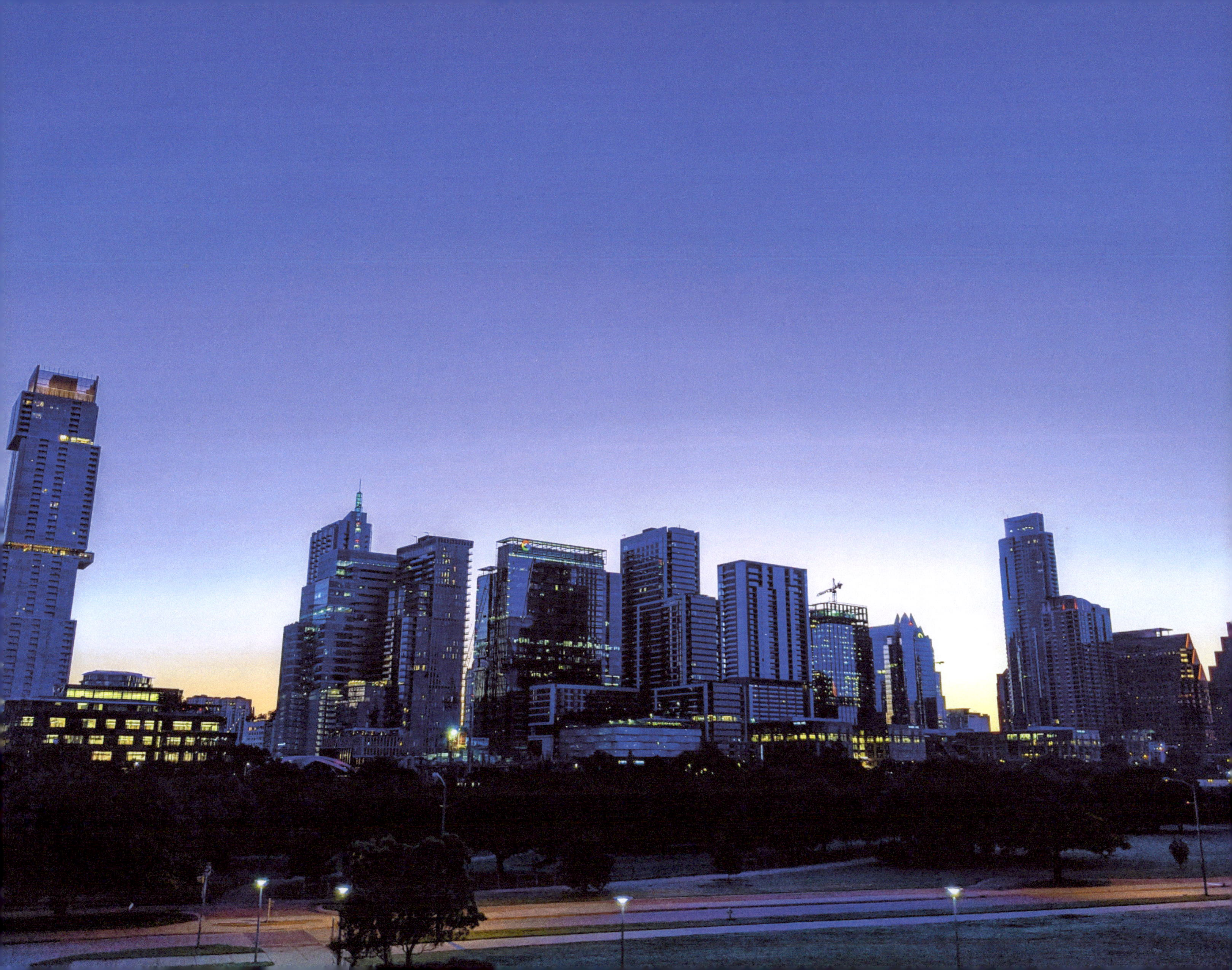

The remnants contrasted by the return of the day.

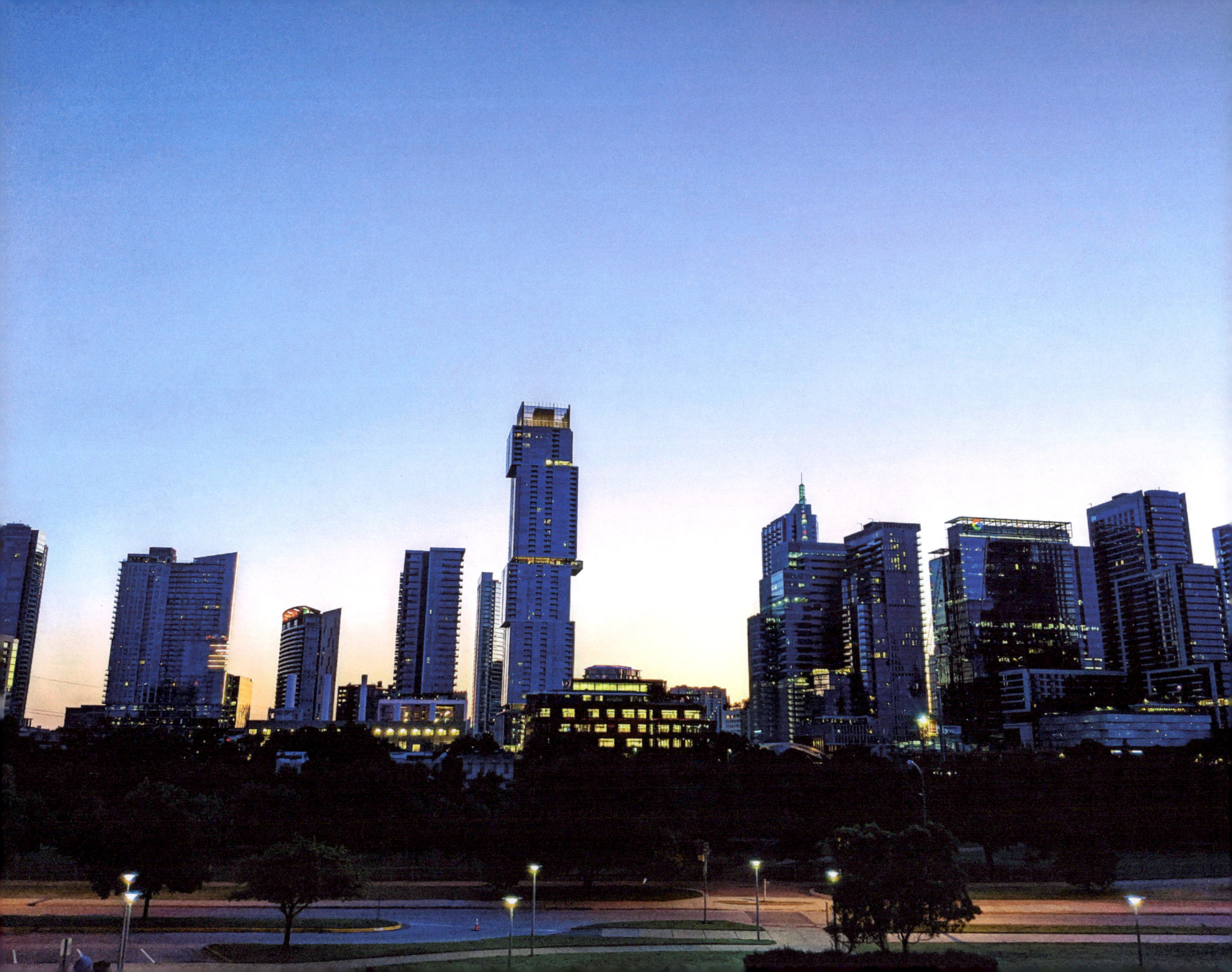

What's left of the black turns to orange and blue, while the sun
resumes its course…

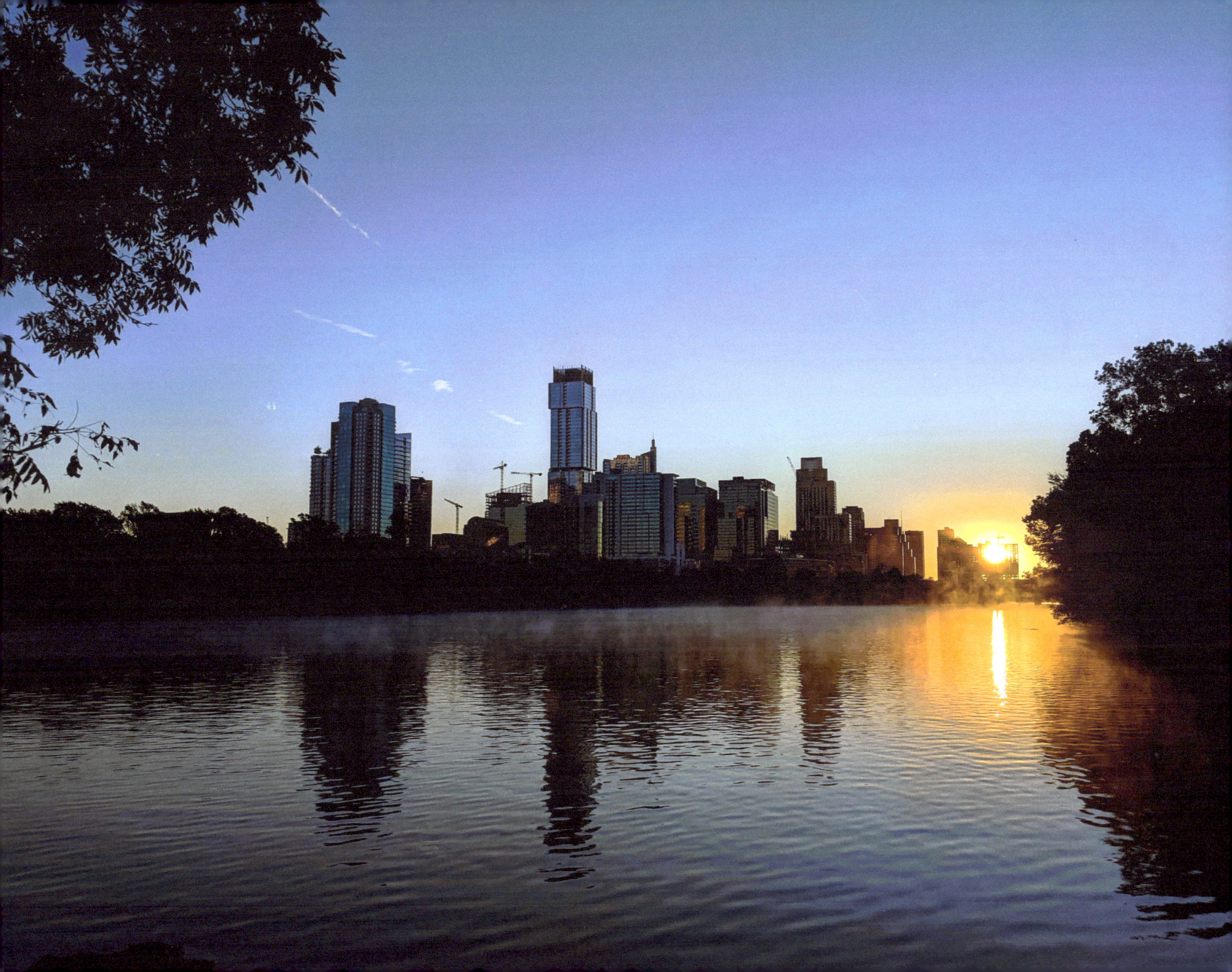

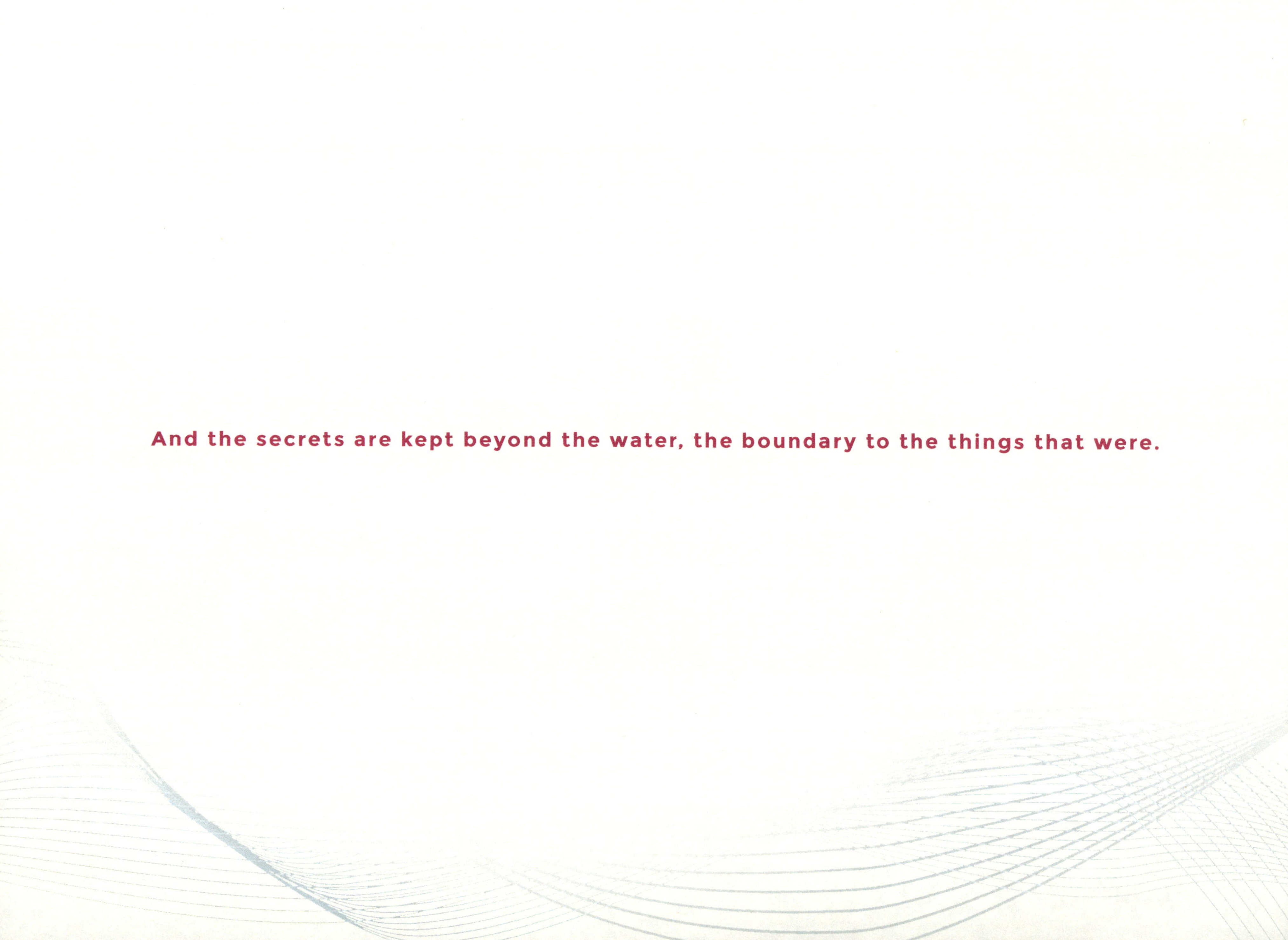

And the secrets are kept beyond the water, the boundary to the things that were.

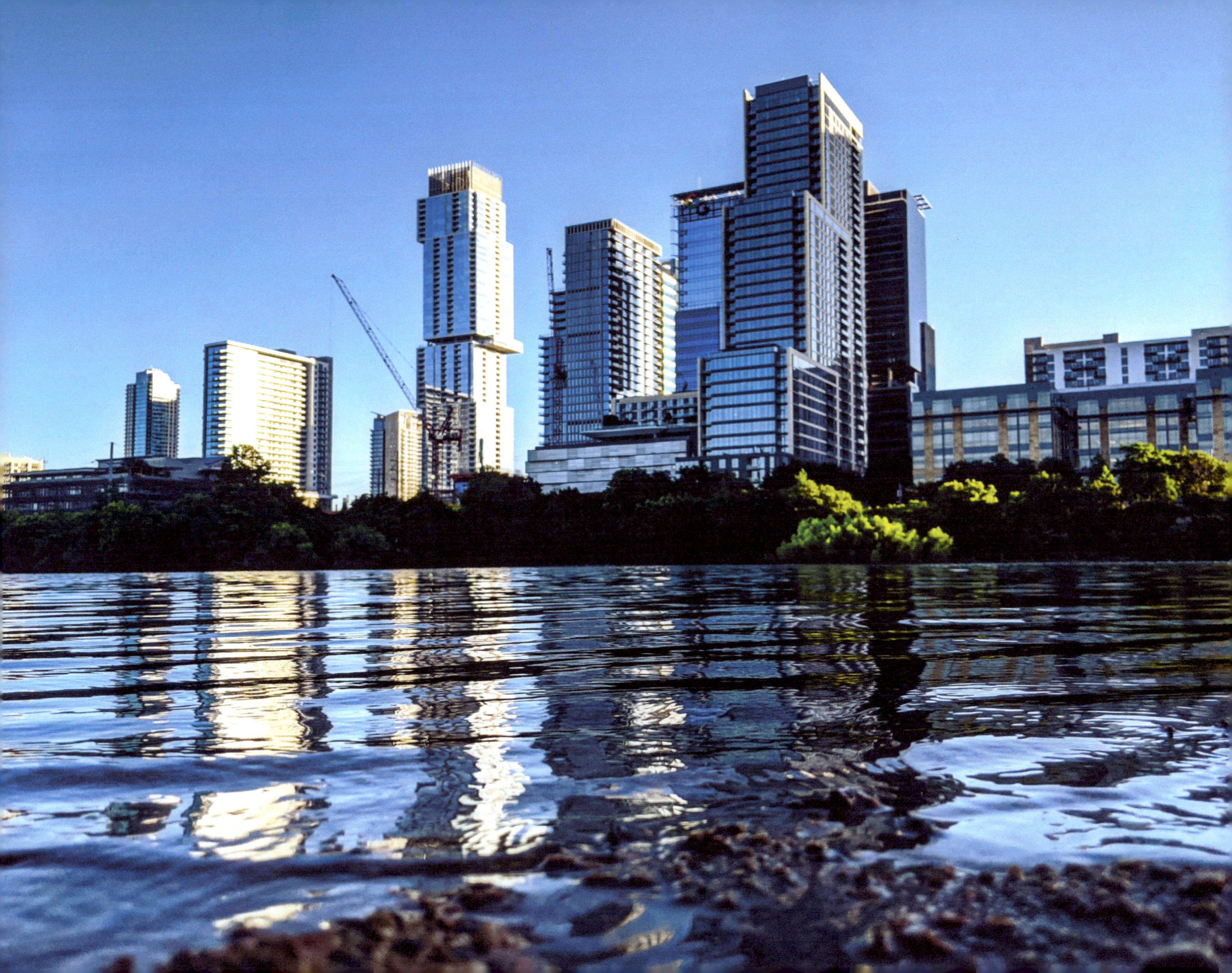

In this city, one can be completely anonymous, yet never far from home.

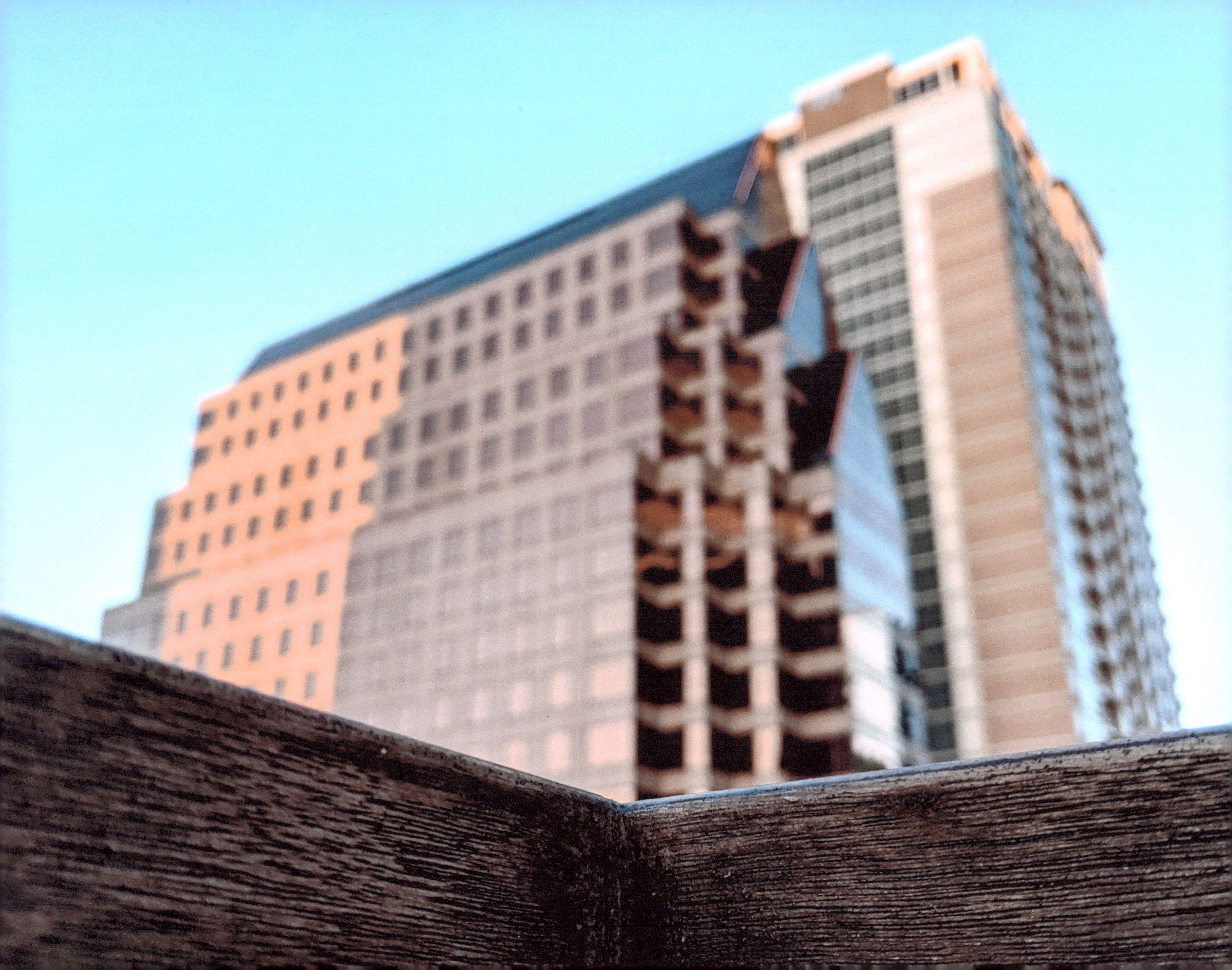

In this city, the towers stand tall. Powered by their own electric fire.

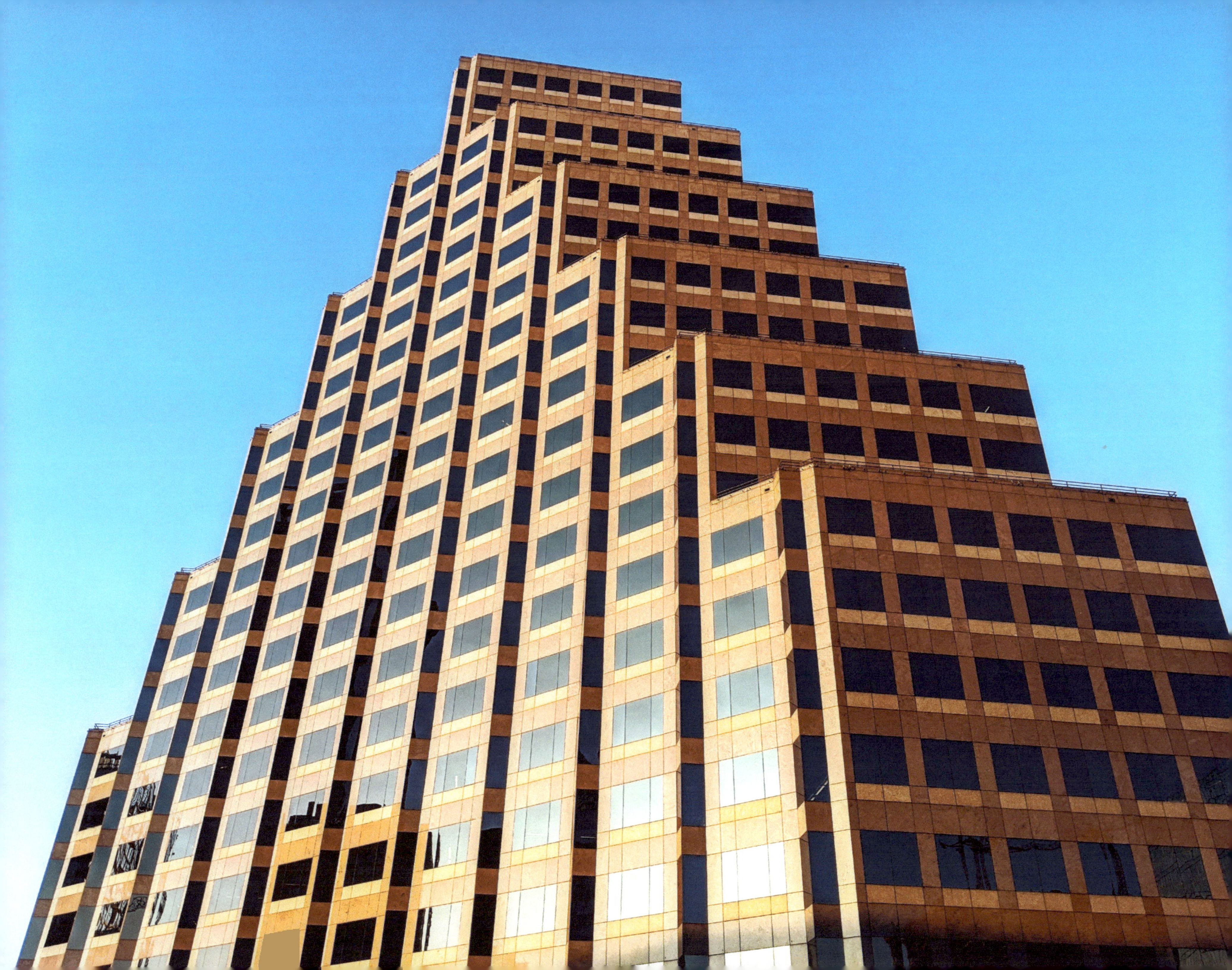

Some things may be different, and yet vaguely familiar.

Some places faintly remembered…

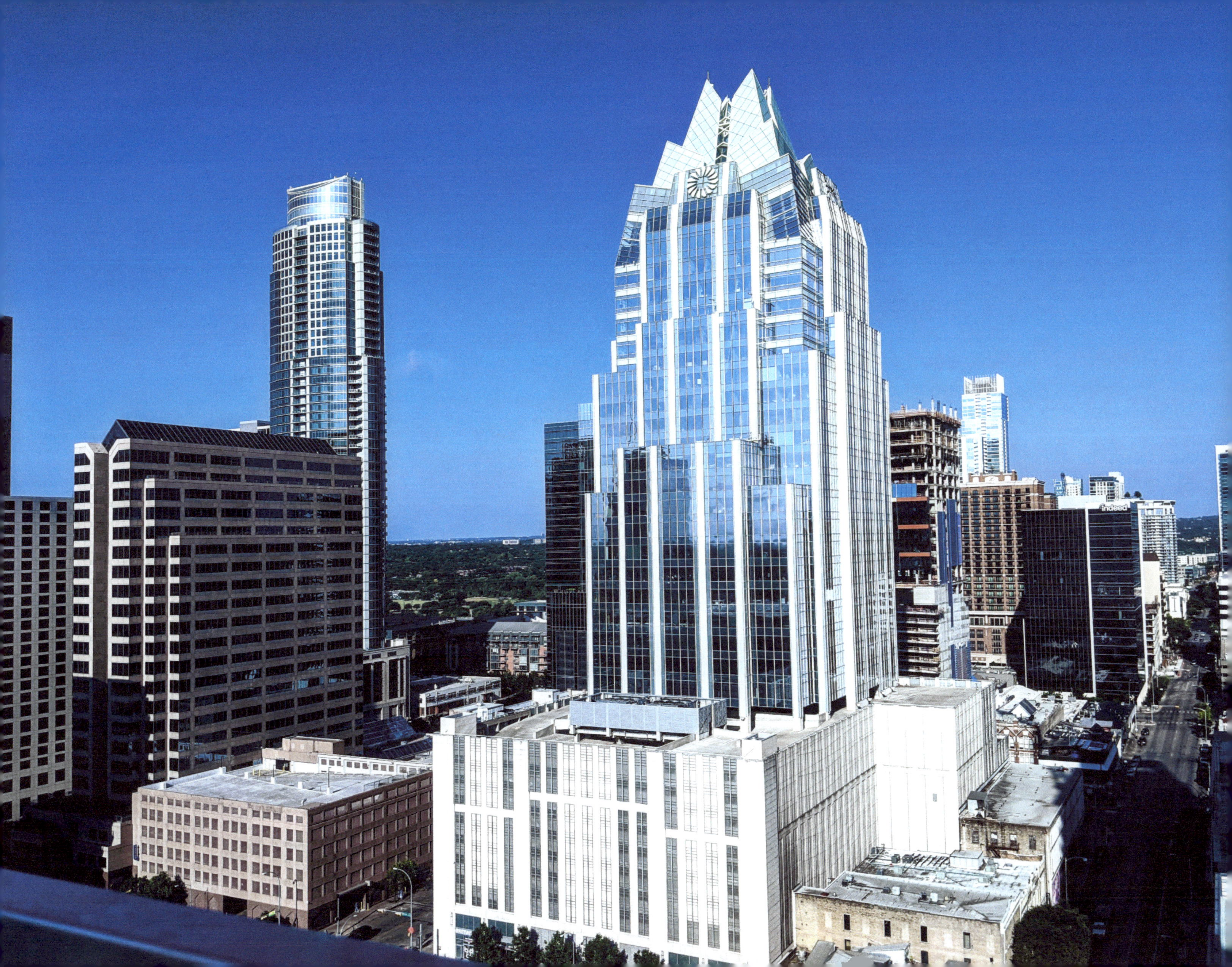

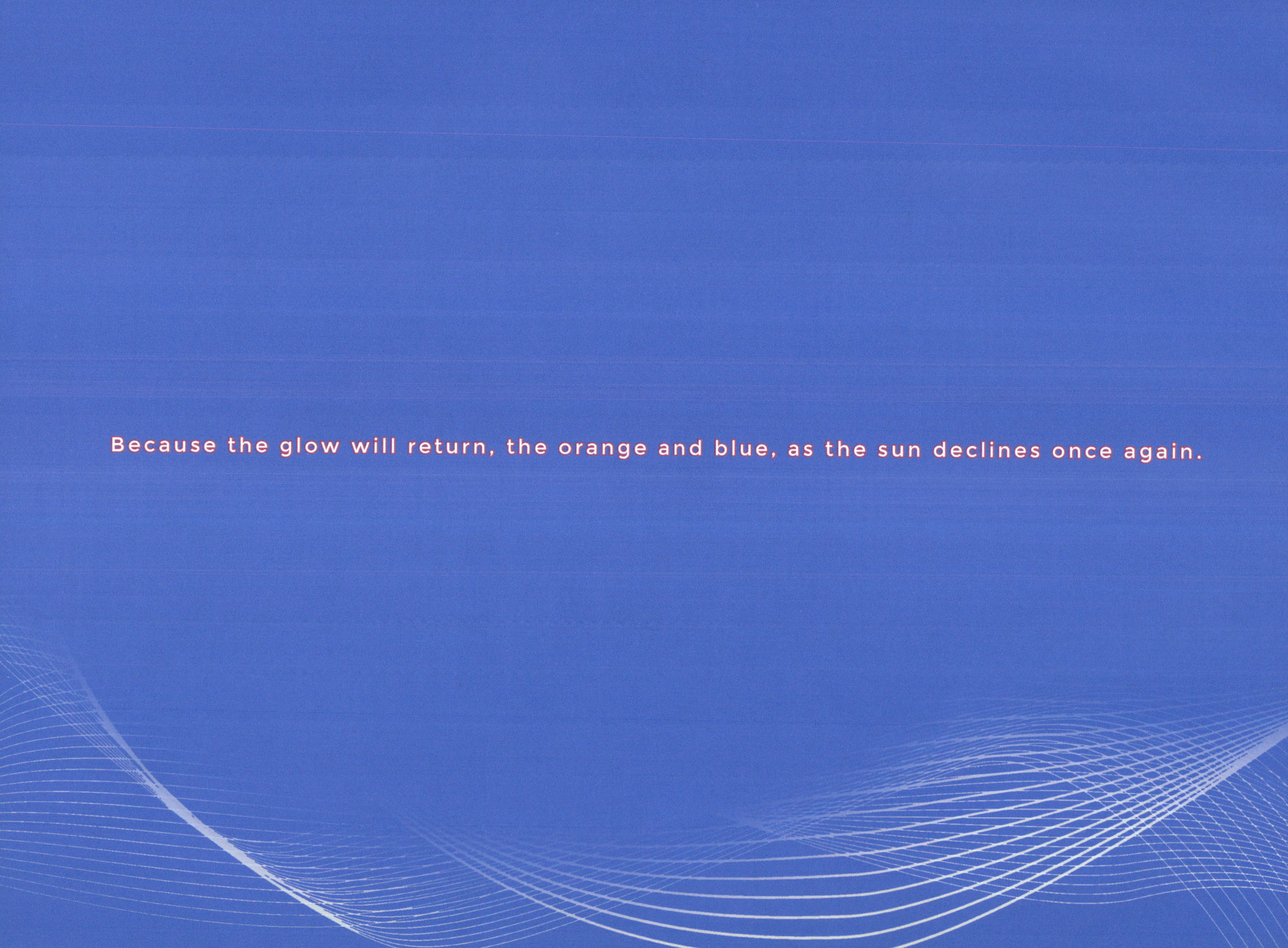
Because the glow will return, the orange and blue, as the sun declines once again.

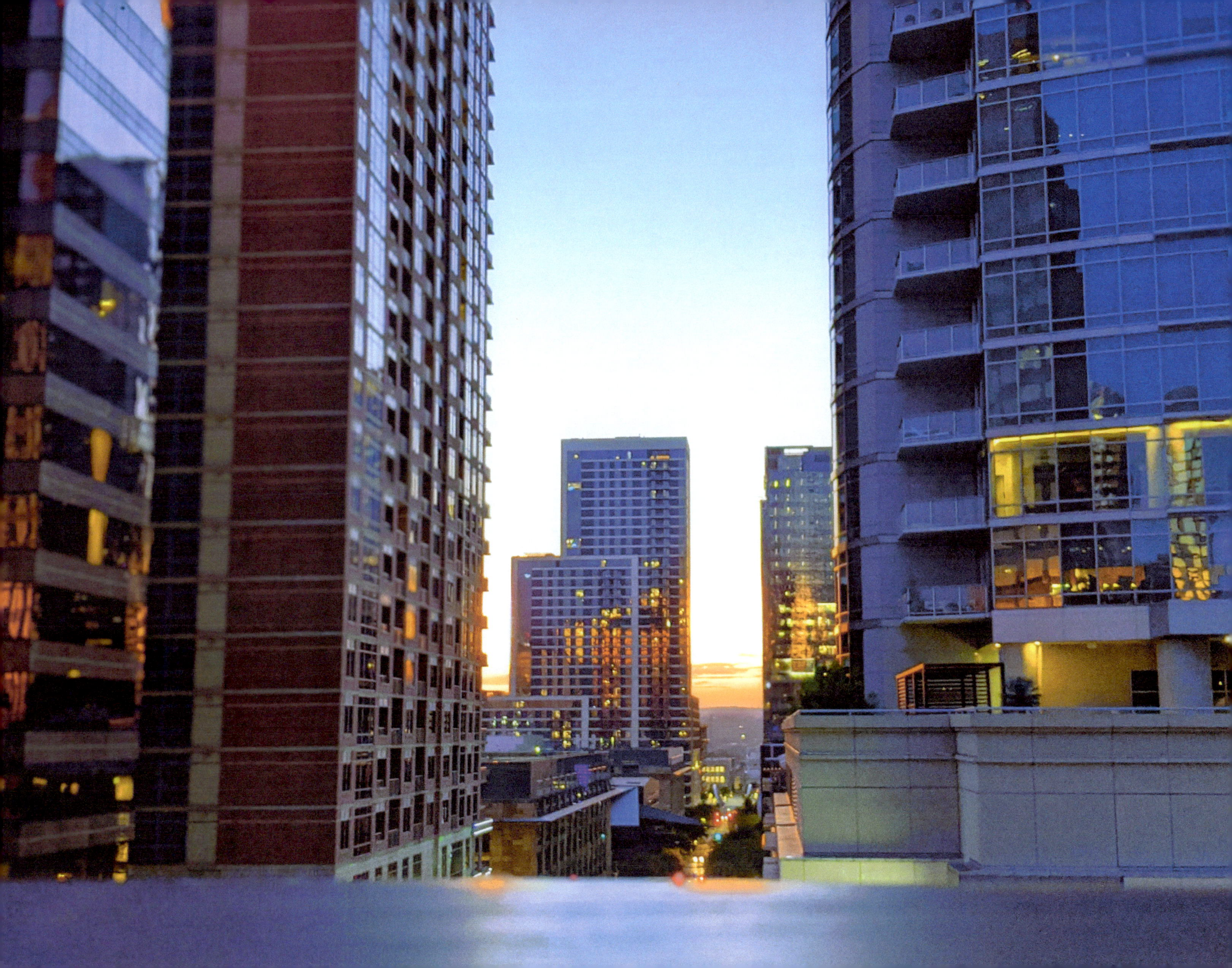

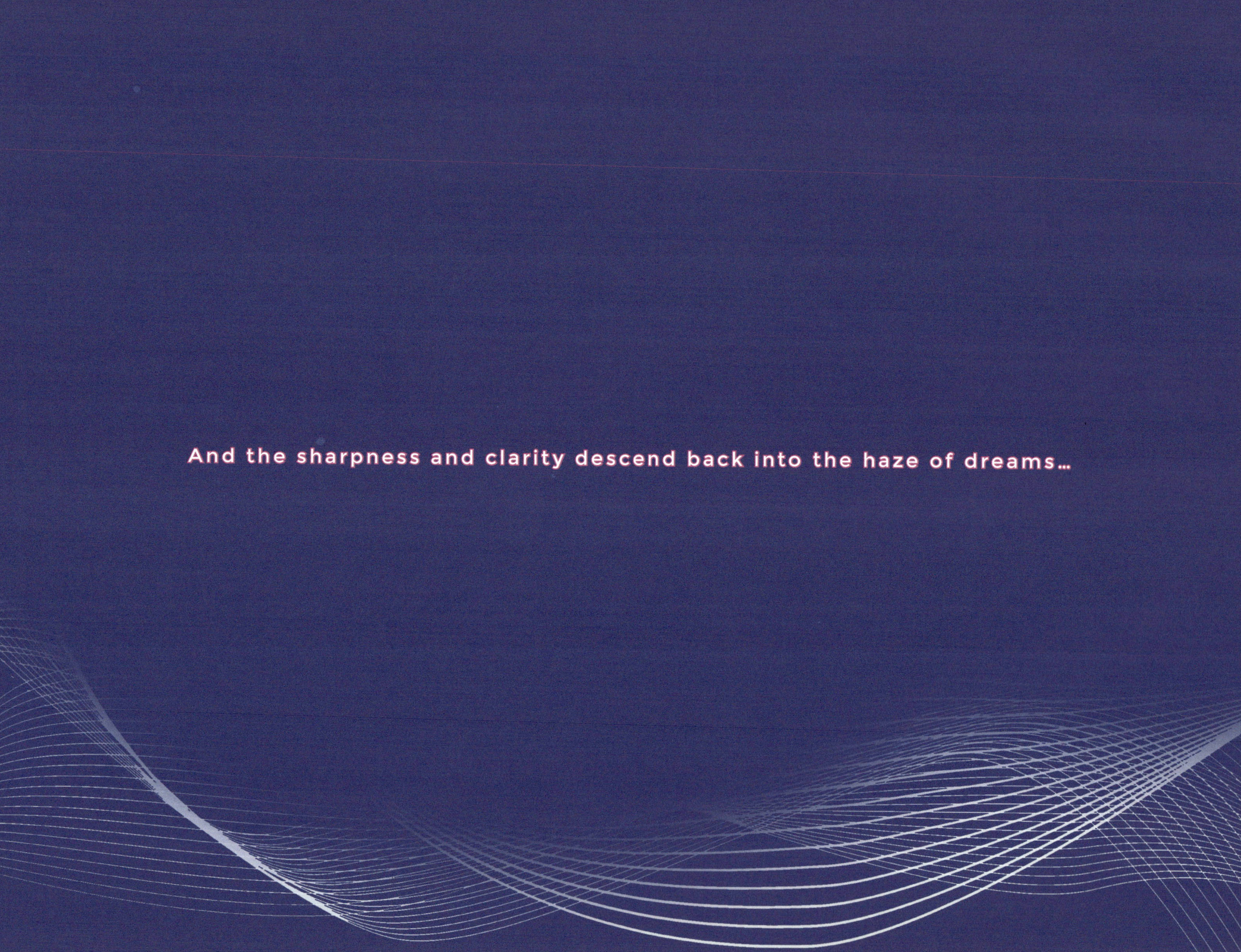

And the sharpness and clarity descend back into the haze of dreams…

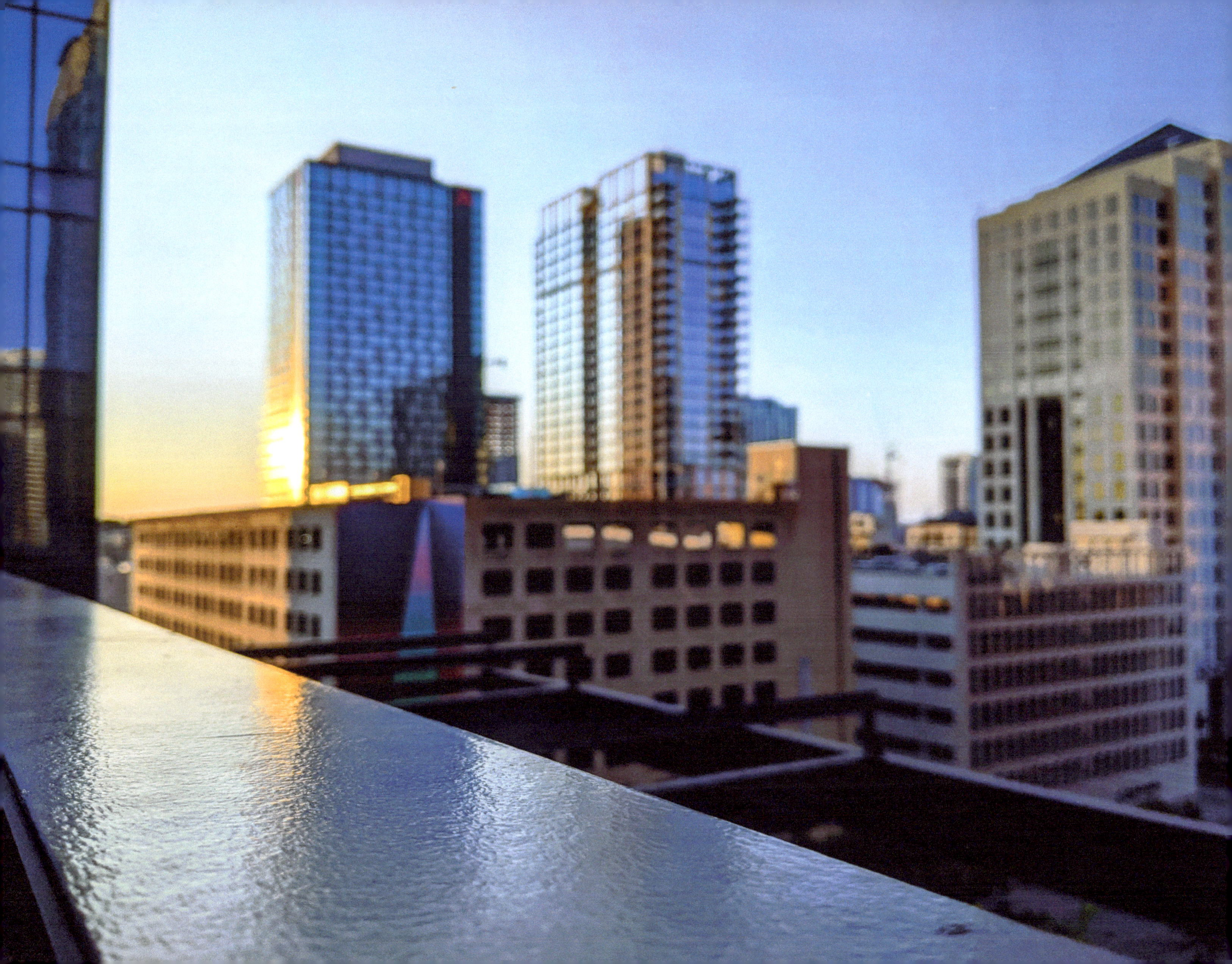

Don't lose the love to be here, even if you were born to leave.

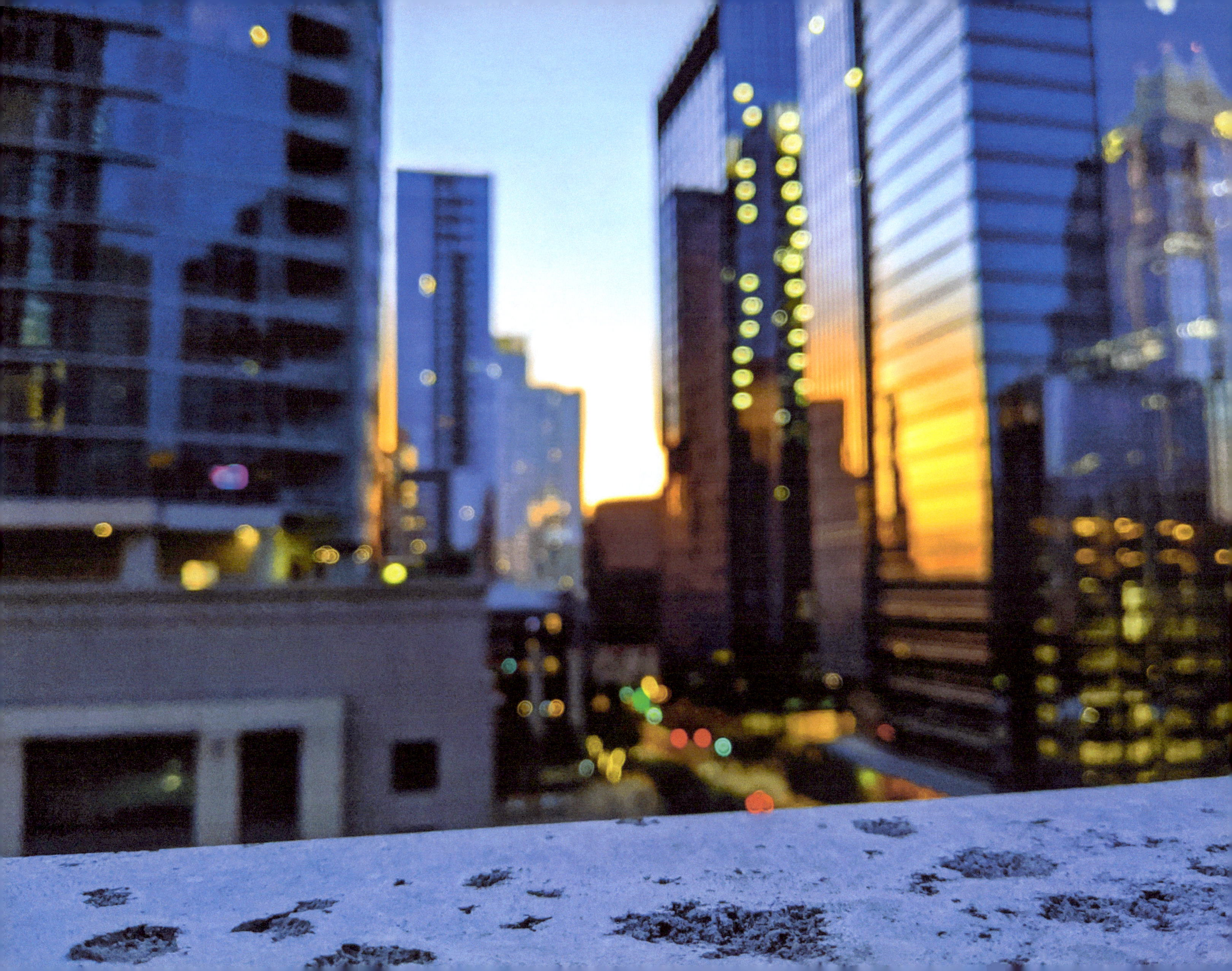

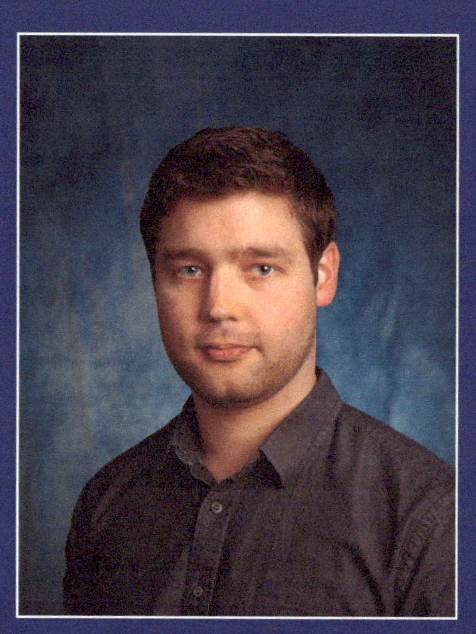

ABOUT THE AUTHOR

Nick Stockland is a Texas Tech graduate, class of 2012. A young professional in the IT consulting industry, currently living in the greatest city in the world – Austin, Texas. Already the author of several children's books, this is Nick's third endeavor in photography.